FREEDOM'S
UNSTEADY
MARCH

FREEDOM'S UNSTEADY MARCH

America's Role in Building Arab Democracy

TAMARA COFMAN WITTES

BROOKINGS INSTITUTION PRESS
Washington, D.C.

Library of Congress Cataloging-in-Publication data

Wittes, Tamara Cofman, 1969–
Freedom's unsteady march : America's role in building Arab democracy / Tamara
Cofman Wittes.
    p.   cm.
Summary: "Dissects the Bush administration's failure to advance freedom in the
Middle East. Lays out a strategy for committed U.S. promotion of democracy, arguing
that only development of a more liberal and democratic politics in the Arab world can
create a firmer foundation for Arab-American ties and secure U.S. long-term goals"—
Provided by publisher.
    Includes bibliographical references and index.
    ISBN 978-0-8157-9494-3 (cloth : alk. paper)
1. Democracy—Middle East. 2. Democratization—Middle East. 3. Middle East—
Foreign relations—United States. 4. United States—Foreign relations—Middle East.
I. Title.
JQ1758.A91W58 2008
327.56073—dc22   2008001999

9 8 7 6 5 4 3 2 1

The paper used in this publication meets minimum requirements of the
American National Standard for Information Sciences—Permanence of Paper
for Printed Library Materials: ANSI Z39.48-1992.

Typeset in Minion

Composition by Cynthia Stock
Silver Spring, Maryland

Printed by R. R. Donnelley
Harrisonburg, Virginia

Contents

Foreword

"DEMOCRACY" IS AMONG the most sacred words in the vocabulary of American politics—and American foreign policy as well. The Founding Fathers believed theirs was a new kind of nation, one based on the principle that the individual has inalienable rights, that the citizenry is self-governing, that leaders answer to the people rather than the other way around. Since that principle was held to be universal, it has often been reflected in American diplomacy and in the dispatch of American armed forces to far corners of the world. That has especially been the case since the late nineteenth century, when the United States emerged as a global power. An early example was Woodrow Wilson's vow that America's entry into the Great War would make the world safe for democracy. Less than two decades ago, with the erosion and collapse of a totalitarian ideology in the Soviet Union and dictatorships giving way to elected leaders in Latin America, democracy seemed to be sweeping the world. The nineties saw bipartisan support in the U.S. Congress for the Freedom Support Act, which was intended to help former Soviet bloc countries develop independent judiciaries, healthy civil societies, pluralistic electoral politics, and the other prerequisites for their transformation into successful modern countries.

In recent years, however, "democracy" has become a controversial if not dirty word in many parts of the world. In Russia, it is often turned into a scatological pun and treated as a synonym for political chaos, economic inequality, and self-righteous American interference in Russia's internal affairs. In Latin America, especially in the Andean region, a demagogic brand of populism has a hero in Hugo Chávez.

But the single greatest setback to democracy promotion as a cornerstone of American foreign policy has been George W. Bush's invocation of that goal in Iraq and in the Greater Middle East. Few scholars understand what has happened—and why, what it means, and what to do about it—as well as Tamara Wittes, a senior fellow in the Saban Center at Brookings. As she demonstrates in the pages that follow, Bush's Freedom Agenda faltered in the Arab world because of the instability unleashed by the invasion of Iraq. In part, that was because of the recalcitrance of Arab autocrats. But the administration also failed to take account of risks to American interests and let itself be lulled into believing that the toppling of a tyrant in Baghdad would vindicate a benign version of the domino theory throughout the region.

Tamara puts the folly of Iraq in the broader context of the tension between the best of American intentions and the worst of consequences. In particular, she analyzes earlier cases where the actual or prospective rise of Islamist political movements has tended to make Washington more deferential to autocratic regimes. This phenomenon is part of a global and long-standing pattern. During the cold war, American presidents would often back a dictator—a Somoza in Nicaragua, the Shah of Iran—if he seemed to be serving as a bulwark against Soviet inroads in a strategically vital region. It was about Somoza that Franklin Roosevelt famously remarked, "He's a son of a bitch, but he's our son of a bitch"—and that was before the cold war. FDR's line is a translation into American idiom of an Arab proverb, "The enemy of my enemy is my friend."

Tamara deconstructs carefully and convincingly the tangle of conflicting considerations that have guided, and too often misguided, U.S. policy in the Middle East. American officials have frequently shied away from pressing their Arab counterparts on human rights for fear that they would lose Arab cooperation on gulf security, energy issues, and the Middle East peace process. Tamara believes that the failure to date of democracy in the Arab world may be due not only to the "exceptionalism" of Arab oil sheikdoms and revolutionary republics—their unexpected resistance to democratizing trends that have swept every other region of the globe—but also to the U.S.'s readiness to grant its Arab allies an exemption from America's advocacy of human rights and democracy.

While recognizing the dilemmas posed by consistent support for those goals, Tamara forcefully rejects the notion—all too commonly held—that the Arab world prefers autocratic rule and "isn't ready for" democracy. She cites polls indicating that the peoples of the Middle East desire political freedom as much as those in other parts of the world. Tamara makes a powerful case on behalf of continued American efforts to advance Arab democracy, arguing that in most Arab countries, the risks of trying to maintain a shaky status quo may be even greater than the risks of a democratic transition.

For the United States to help shepherd the growth of freedom in this region, Tamara argues that it must overcome the deep-seated American ambivalence about Arab democracy. Her sharp insights show us how to do just that. She has tracked Bush's Freedom Agenda since its inception through dogged data gathering and numerous interviews with government officials and local Arab activists. She draws on this knowledge to build a clear-eyed examination of the Bush record and to illuminate the relationship between Arab political development and American foreign policy. With sober judgment, she suggests ways to reconcile the apparent conflicts between democracy promotion and America's other pressing strategic concerns in the Middle East, identifying priorities and picking a path across a tumultuous landscape whereby the United States can promote its values while protecting its interests in this volatile but crucial region.

Tamara looks ahead to the challenge facing the next administration, which—in part because of the failure of Bush's Freedom Agenda—may find it difficult to win support for continued American efforts to advance democratic growth worldwide. Tamara gives us—to borrow a phrase from the diplomacy of the Middle East—a road map that might avoid this trap.

This book is just the latest example of the work Tamara has done at the Saban Center, where she directs the Project on Middle East Democracy and Development. I'm proud to have her as a colleague at Brookings, and the Saban Center is proud to sponsor this timely and important work.

STROBE TALBOTT
President

January 2008
Washington, D.C.

Acknowledgments

M
Y THANKS ARE due first and foremost to Martin Indyk and Ken
Pollack, of the Saban Center at Brookings, for their wisdom in
identifying this topic early on as one worthy of serious attention
and for their trust in giving me space to delve into the work. I am likewise
indebted to the founding donors of the Saban Center, Haim and Cheryl
Saban, and to all the center's supporters, for making my work possible. Todd
G. Patkin and the Hewlett Foundation merit special thanks for supporting
my efforts as director of the Saban Center's Project on Middle East Democracy and Development. The Brookings Institution's unparalleled support
for independent intellectual work on tough policy questions makes it an
ideal home; I am grateful to Brookings president Strobe Talbott and vice
president for foreign policy studies Carlos Pascual for their leadership in
nurturing a uniquely edifying environment in which I could pursue the
questions at the heart of this book.

My research assistants during the preparation of the book, Sarah Yerkes
and Andrew Masloski, merit immense reward and recognition for their yeo-
man's labor; I can at least provide the latter here. Laura Mooney and Sarah
Chilton at the Brookings library provided swift and expert assistance track-
ing down sources. Janet Walker's editorial guidance and Jane Kepp's skillful
copyediting smoothed the path to press.

Countless Arab and American officials and civic activists informed my
analysis through in-person conversations and by allowing me to observe

their work up close. I am grateful to all of them, including those who are not named in these pages. Michele Dunne, Peter Berkowitz, Dan Byman, Josh Muravchik, Jonathan Rauch, Ellen Lust-Okar, Carlos Pascual, Ken Pollack, and two anonymous reviewers provided comments on the manuscript. I am indebted to all of them for their time and insights. Others who endured my incoherence, provided insights that shaped my thinking, and offered fellowship, sound advice, and warm spirits to buoy me throughout the research, writing, and revisions were Ammar Abdulhamid, Jon Alterman, Nathan Brown, Dan Brumberg, Les Campbell, Scott Carpenter, Rola Dashti, Navtej Dhillon, Greg Gause, Phil Gordon, Karim Haggag, Steve Heydemann, Sameer Jarrah, Rami Khouri, Martin Kramer, Suzanne Maloney, Mike McFaul, Ellen McHugh, Marwan Muasher, Bruce Riedel, Jeremy Shapiro, Emad Tinawi, and Tarek Yousef.

Like most authors, I relied heavily on my family's patience and loving support as I wrote this book. My husband, Ben, is my best booster as well as my best editor. He gave me time to work while somehow producing two books of his own during the same period. Clearly, I still have a great deal to learn from him, and I am grateful every day for his willingness to teach me.

My grandparents, Bruce and Joan Millen, believed in a principled American internationalism, helped to nurture my early interest in international affairs, and served as an eager audience for my evolving views on democracy in the Middle East. They lived the last years of their lives just a few blocks from the Brookings Institution, where my grandfather had himself been a visiting fellow and author of a Brookings book. I regret that neither of them lived to see this book's completion, and I dedicate it to their honored memory.

CHAPTER ONE

The End of Arab
Exceptionalism, and
of America's Own

T HE FINAL YEAR of the George W. Bush administration admittedly presents an awkward context for a book arguing for a muscular American policy of democracy promotion in the Middle East. Attempting to push the Middle East toward more American-style government was, after all, one of the Bush administration's hallmarks, and the results have discredited the project as few could have imagined. Where the administration failed, it failed spectacularly. The overthrow of Saddam Hussein in Iraq produced a seemingly endless military quagmire that resulted in thousands of dead American soldiers and untold numbers of dead Iraqis; the reconstruction effort produced nothing an American might confuse with democracy. Even where the administration succeeded by its own terms, it failed spectacularly. It pushed for elections in the Palestinian territories and got a Hamas government and a civil war among the Palestinian factions. It pushed for fairer and more open elections in Egypt and got a show of electoral force from the Muslim Brotherhood. It pushed for new elections in Lebanon, free from Syrian meddling, and got an impressive showing by Hizballah and a weak and paralyzed government whose collapse it has had to struggle ever since to prevent. Given these outcomes, many Americans now regard the promotion of democracy as a fool's errand, the province of naïfs and neoconservatives. Even Secretary of State Condoleezza Rice, who so boldly championed Middle East democracy, has practically stopped talking about it except when asked by a journalist.

So it is with full awareness of the uphill climb I face with most readers that I state what should be an unremarkable thesis: promoting democracy in the Arab world remains an imperative for the United States. This is the case not merely—or even mainly—because democracy might act as an antidote to the spread of Islamist terrorism but because enduring American interests in the region require us to embrace and advance democracy for Arab citizens. America's fundamental interests in the Middle East remain largely unchanged, despite the dramatic threats revealed by the attacks of September 11, 2001, and despite the massive, costly, and long-term intervention in Iraq. What has changed, radically, is the effectiveness of America's traditional means of securing its regional interests. What has worked in the past will not work in the future.

In the coming years the United States will find its historical tools of alliance-building in the Middle East altogether insufficient to protect American interests. As the Iraq war has amply shown, even America's overwhelming military power does not enable it to achieve its regional goals unilaterally. U.S.-Arab cooperation remains a fundamental necessity for regional peace and global economic stability. But the path to promoting and sustaining successful cooperation has irrevocably changed. U.S.-Arab cooperation can no longer be sustained on the crumbling foundation of the past—the reliance on strong, autocratic leaders who can guarantee policy cooperation even in the face of domestic disapproval. A stable new basis for America's necessary regional engagement can be built only on the enlightened self-interest of both sides, and today, unlike in the past, that requires the consent of the region's citizens. Only the development of liberal democracies in the Arab world's major states will, in the long term, secure the advancement of American goals in the region.

The Middle East is, according to Freedom House, the least democratic region on the globe. It resisted even the third wave of democratization that swept through Asia, Latin America, and eastern Europe during the 1980s and 1990s. Arab "exceptionalism" has produced its own scholarly literature of explanation and apology.[1] Scholars have explained the persistence of Arab authoritarianism through reference to historical circumstances, religious philosophy, political culture, great-power politics, and oil economics, among other factors.[2] Over the decades since the collapse of the Ottoman Empire following its defeat in World War I, Arab states have been through many waves of political upheaval, yet the Arab world has not witnessed a single successful transition to democracy. A number of regimes in the region survive essentially unaltered from their form at the moment of postcolonial independence. But most Arab regimes have undergone dramatic changes, including revolution, civil war, and military rule. More recently, since the end of the cold war, many Arab rulers have experimented with reforms in economics, politics, or both. They have used the banner of "democratization" to refer to the reestablishment of parliamentary bodies (Kuwait), the revision of press and association laws (Jordan and Egypt), and the holding of contested presidential elections (Yemen). Indeed, at several points in the past twenty years, the relatively quick pace and broad scope of reforms in certain countries led observers to hail a democratic transformation in the region. But by and large these changes amounted to little improvement in the distribution of political power in Arab societies or in the minimal degree of public accountability governments in the region enjoy.

In recent years the rhetoric of democratization and the use of certain of democracy's forms have been in vogue even among Arab autocrats. Four of the conservative tribal monarchies of the Arab gulf have given women the right to vote and run for office.[3] Egypt's long-time autocrat, President Hosni Mubarak, allowed himself to be reelected to his fifth term through a competitive ballot rather than, as in previous years, a yes-or-no referendum.[4] At the sixth annual Doha Forum on Democracy, Development, and Free Trade, held in April 2006, the Qatari emir, hereditary monarch of the tiny gulf nation, said that "the success of the democratic process is essential for addressing the manifestations of tyranny and corruption that still devour the people's fortunes, deprive them of their rights, and push some of them to extremism and alienation."[5] Even the calcified Arab League agreed, in March 2004, to "keep pace with the rapid world changes, by consolidating the democratic practice, by enlarging participation in political and public life, [and] by fostering the role of all components of the civil society, including NGOs, in conceiving of the guidelines of the society of tomorrow."[6]

The most dramatic change in rhetoric, however, has come not from the region but from the White House. Many commentators greeted President Bush's commitment, declared in November 2003, to spreading democracy in the Middle East as a radical restructuring of American policy toward the region. But the commitment was not entirely new; the administration's rhetorical emphasis on transforming the politics of the Arab world had been evident since shortly after the 9/11 attacks. At West Point in June 2002, for example, the president asserted, "The twentieth century ended with a single surviving model of human progress, based on non-negotiable demands of human dignity, the rule of law, limits on the power of the state, respect for women and private property and free speech and equal justice and religious tolerance. . . . Mothers and fathers and children across the Islamic world, and all the world, share the same fears and aspirations."[7]

Seven months later, on the eve of the Iraq war, the president argued the importance of democratization in the Arab world for American security, asserting that "stable and free nations do not breed the ideologies of murder."[8] Bush has sustained his rhetorical emphasis on democratization in the years since then. In his second inaugural address he famously declared, "The survival of liberty in our land increasingly depends on the success of liberty in other lands. The best hope for peace in our world is the expansion of freedom in all the world."[9] And in a speech at the National Defense University in March 2005 he said that "for the sake of our long-term security, all free nations must stand with the forces of democracy and justice that have begun to transform the Middle East."[10]

The reason for this shift in presidential attitudes toward Middle East autocracy is an altered view of international security and its requirements that derives from the end of the cold war and the rise of transnational security threats, including international organized crime, refugee and other migrant flows, and, most notably, international terrorism.[11] If events such as the Rwandan genocide or the Somali state's collapse demonstrated the consequences of internal political dynamics for the security of neighboring states, then the al Qaeda attacks of September 11, 2001, drove home to many Western leaders the idea that domestic politics in one country or region might produce consequences affecting the security of states far distant.[12]

The U.S. government thus embraced the necessity of democratizing the Middle East in order to, as the phrase goes, "drain the swamp" from which Islamist terrorism emerges.[13] The president's "forward strategy of freedom" was the first attempt by the Bush administration to enunciate a positive vision for American engagement in the post-Saddam Middle East. It was also, quite consciously, a strategy for winning the war on terrorism by transforming the dysfunctional politics of the region, which in Bush's view made Arab citizens resentful and repressed and so more vulnerable to the appeals of extremist ideology. The Freedom Agenda, as the administration formally dubbed it, was billed as the political face of America's counterterrorism effort. Deeper and more meaningful than any attempt to "win hearts and minds" for the United States itself, it was an effort to win Arab hearts and minds over to the practice of American values and virtues—whether the new practitioners ultimately embraced the United States and its policies or not. From this perspective the goal of democracy in the Arab and broader Muslim worlds was to marginalize Islamist extremists, delegitimate political violence, and so make the world safe for Americans.

President Bush was probably correct in supposing that spreading liberal values in the Middle East would reduce the prevalence of anti-American terrorism in the long run. It is hard to imagine that, embraced by Arab societies, values such as toleration, limited government, individual rights, and equality before the law would not help to limit the appeal of the ideology— deeply intolerant, totalitarian, even nihilistic—that undergirds the terrorists' actions and provides them with moral, popular, and financial support and with a pool of willing recruits. Although democracy might not defeat terrorism, in the long run it ought to help undermine the popularity of violent, radical Islamism in countries where the ideology currently enjoys followers, sympathizers, and admirers.[14]

The trouble is that although this theory has strong philosophical roots and many friends, it is as yet entirely speculative.[15] Democratic societies produce terrorism and recently have even produced Islamist terrorists such as, to name only a few examples, Zacarias Moussaoui, Richard Reid, and the perpetrators of the July 2005 attacks on the London subway. Democratization, moreover, is a long-term and uncertain process and, as recent scholarship has shown, often produces violence.[16] The assumption that democratization could defeat terrorism seems a thin reed upon which to build such a dramatic new commitment for American foreign policy.

But here is the rub: Although George W. Bush's application of America's traditional democratic idealism to the Middle East may derive largely from the post-9/11 logic of the global war on terror, it also responds, intentionally or not, to a real and growing crisis in Middle East governance. The hesitant reforms of the Arab world's monarchs and imperial presidents and the mounting domestic and international pressure for more reform both respond to Arab societies' sinking circumstances in a changed global environment. In a world in which democratic governance is an increasingly universal norm, in which political, social, and economic openness and flexibility appear to be the keys to successful development, the Arab states are increasingly out of step.[17] At the same time, demographic forces within the Arab countries are increasingly challenging their governments' abilities to provide the basics: education, housing, health care, and jobs. The governance crisis in the Arab states has deep and long-standing roots. And the forces of change that are buffeting the Middle East from within and without are strong and growing.

They are not, by and large, explicitly democratic forces, meaning that the outcome of the coming change, without some concerted push, may well not be democratic either. Indeed, democratization in the Middle East is by no means inevitable—it is a very uncertain path, fraught with danger. But it is a path that the peoples of the Middle East must take, because the alternatives are so much worse—for them, for us, and for the world.

Because of this reality, America's new policy of democracy promotion in the Arab world is not best viewed as a naïve, ideological juggernaut that deserves to crash and burn with the end of Bush's second term in office. Rather, the policy meshes with the real historical circumstances of both domestic and regional Arab politics. Bush's policy commitment to Arab democracy was significant not because it promised an end to Islamist terrorism—which it could not realistically hope to deliver—but because it was responsive to historical developments already under way in the Middle East. That is why getting American policy right on this issue is so important and why the actual execution of the Freedom Agenda has been so disappointing.

Indeed, despite the high-volume rhetorical commitments of the Bush administration, it remains to be seen whether the United States can help to midwife the birth of a democratic Arab future or whether, if the transformation occurs, the United States will be a mere spectator. The structures put into place to implement President Bush's Freedom Agenda for the Middle East were woefully inadequate to the task at hand, and the minimal investments of funds and, more important, of political capital made by the United States in supporting Arab democrats have so far had little effect other than threatening the credibility of the project.

Already in the Freedom Agenda's first few years the project has been beset by a lack of commitment among the foreign policy bureaucracy, by a mismatch between the assistance strategy and realities on the ground, and, most notably, by a lack of sufficient support at senior policy levels to bolster democracy assistance with frank government-to-government dialogue. A degree of naïveté in designing and implementing programs also limited the policy's force and chipped away at its effectiveness and the seriousness with which rulers and activists in the region viewed it. Continuing down this path risks undermining the foundation of American public and congressional support for the larger project.

America's weak-kneed policy, though, does not result simply from indecision or an inadequate commitment to democratization on Bush's part. It flows, rather, from genuine dilemmas and costs associated with the promotion of democracy—costs vividly on display in the Hamas victory and the gains by Islamists in Egypt and militants in Lebanon. The United States, while it today enjoys unprecedented and perhaps unmatched ability to influence the direction of change in the Arab Middle East, still faces significant risks and obstacles to doing so effectively. First is the potential for democratic processes in Arab states to produce outcomes that many Americans, including many policymakers, find unpalatable—specifically, the election of Islamists to the leaderships of what are today friendly Arab states. Second is the possibility that a serious-minded pro-democracy policy might impede Arab regimes' cooperation with Washington on other issues of importance. These two factors, along with other challenges of policy implementation, explain the hesitation and half-measures that have characterized even the most aggressive American efforts to advance democracy in this region.

The ambivalence these risks and costs induce is understandable, but it creates a major impediment of its own: a significant credibility deficit on America's part in arguing for democratic change to an Arab audience. Grassroots activists know the difference between drop-in-the-bucket grant-making programs administered by mid-level bureaucrats and a speech in which the president of the United States demands, as Ronald Reagan did of Mikhail Gorbachev in Berlin, that the Soviet leader "tear down this wall." And America's limited credibility with the Arab public, in any event, impairs its ability to play a direct role in encouraging grassroots democratic development. Indeed, some Arab democracy activists argue that, given America's tainted reputation in the region, direct American assistance harms grassroots democrats more than it helps them. Any effective policy of democracy promotion must begin by confronting and resolving the risks of bad outcomes and competing priorities—and addressing thereby the ambivalence they induce in America's own attitude toward the project.

This is not, I admit, a challenge most commentators and policymakers now wish to tackle. The United States is in the midst of a full-fledged backlash against advancing democracy as a policy objective. Democracy promotion, we are told, is naïve, unachievable, and imperialistic. And even when we win, we end up losing. The conventional wisdom argues instead that we have no choice but to bolster the Middle East's extant autocratic regimes as bulwarks against extremism or at most to promote economic and other gradual reforms as spurs to eventual democratization.

This is exactly the wrong answer.

My purpose in this book is to argue that, notwithstanding the failures of the past several years, America has no viable choice but to wield its power and influence firmly on behalf of democratic reform in the Middle East, alongside other reforms in economics and society. For the United States, and indeed for the rest of the international community, the risks that accompany Arab democratization are at least balanced by, if not overwhelmed by, the risks of failing to act on behalf of democratic development in this strategic part of the world. Propping up corrupt autocrats might seem the only way to hold back radical Islamists whom democracy would hasten to power. But, in fact, failing to press assertively for basic political rights serves to entrench the Islamists' position as the sole viable opposition to the autocrats, just as surely as it entrenches the autocrats—for now, at least—in power. Only by pushing to expand political freedoms can the United States cultivate the sort of political movements that can challenge the Islamists for legitimacy as voices of dissent. In pressing for expanded political rights, the United States has more powerful tools than many policymakers and commentators imagine.

All this may seem an obtuse argument given the extent to which, in the public discourse both in the United States and abroad, the Bush administration's policy of advancing Middle Eastern democracy is inextricably linked to the war in Iraq. Yet this conflation misunderstands both the Iraq war and Bush's policy of democracy promotion. Humanitarian intervention to topple a brutal dictatorship was a distant third among the rationales put forward by the Bush administration and its allies for the invasion; the primary arguments had to do with Iraq's weapons of mass destruction, both past and presumed, and its alleged links to terrorist groups. Hope that Saddam's fall would produce a democratic "domino effect" in the region was expressed by the president and other senior officials as a hope, not as a war aim.[18] The United States would not have gone to war simply to create a democracy in Iraq, absent what was then viewed as a compelling security rationale. On the other hand, having made a decision to invade and topple the existing dictatorship, the United States and its allies could not reasonably have been expected to impose a nondemocratic successor regime in Baghdad. The goal of establishing a democratic government in Iraq is properly viewed as a consequence of the decision to go to war, not as a motive.

Similarly, the project of Iraqi stabilization would have been only marginally less difficult had the American military imposed a strongman of its own. The military would still have had to contend with the competing ambitions of Kurds, Sunnis, and Shiites, and it would still have faced an insurgency by al Qaeda and by those dissatisfied with the distribution of power and wealth in post-Saddam Iraq. The challenge of building a democracy in Iraq after the previous regime's defeat is more properly viewed as a project of postconflict reconstruction and nation-building than one of promoting a transition from authoritarianism to democracy.

The Iraq war is a distorted prism through which to view external efforts to cultivate Middle East democracies for another reason: almost no efforts to promote democracy, either today in the Middle East or throughout modern history, have been carried out at the point of a gun. Although international norms clearly endorse democracy as the form of government most protective of fundamental human rights and freedoms, and although post–cold war international practice suggests the evolution of a "duty to protect" citizens from an abusive government as a rationale for external intervention, a lack of democracy in and of itself has *never* been suggested by any state as sufficient reason for military overthrow. Aggravated human rights abuses and transborder effects harmful to international peace and security (such as mass refugee flows) have been required to raise governments' indifference to their citizens to a level worthy of international scrutiny, let alone action.[19] The notion that democracy promotion necessarily involves forcible imposition or military intervention, simply because the war in Iraq did so, is a red herring. Indeed, partly as a result of the fiasco in Iraq, the United States is far from advocating forcible regime change in any other case, either in the Middle East or outside it. The Bush administration may have pressed its relatively ambitious agenda of democracy promotion in the Middle East simultaneous with its execution of the war in Iraq, but the two efforts—except in Iraq itself—employ different approaches and tools. Iraq is not a model of democracy promotion likely ever to be replicated.

This is not to say that the war in Iraq has no implications for efforts to promote democracy in the Middle East. Unfortunately, those implications are vast. At least initially there was some evidence in the wake of the invasion that, as in past episodes of Arab military defeat, Western intervention in the Arab heartland had provoked the sort of introspection that might encourage internal pressures for democratic change. As in 1967, after Israel's lightning defeat of the combined Arab armies and conquest of territory previously held by Syria, Jordan, and Egypt, Arab commentators asked how it was that their nations had become so feeble. The ouster of Saddam likewise compelled even nationalist journalists and intellectuals to ask whether internal weaknesses were what had led to the humiliation of yet another external military intervention in the region. For example, a petition signed by 287 Syrian citizens and delivered to Syrian president Bashar al-Assad in May 2003 noted that "the only force capable" of combating America's imperialist plans in Iraq and Palestine was "a free nation."[20]

More recently, however, the chaos in Iraq has overtaken Arab public perceptions, making an easy case for those who argue for the benefits of order over freedom in public life. It has also further discredited American leadership and, in Arab eyes, motives.[21] This has made it more difficult for those both inside the region and around the world to partner with the United States in advancing Arab democracy. Whether the Iraq war will, in the end, hasten or stymie a democratic trend in the Middle East will be a matter for historians to judge. But however much the American intervention in Iraq may color contemporary perceptions, clearly it is inappropriate to restrict a discussion of the American role in building Arab democracy to an examination of the failed military intervention in Iraq.

The more substantial objection to efforts to promote Arab democracy is that those undertaken by the Bush administration have produced very limited payoffs—and some of the farther-reaching outcomes have yielded profound regret in Washington. The elections in Iraq, Lebanon, and Palestine produced gains by armed Islamist factions whose values are far from the liberal pluralism that the United States would like to see triumph in Arab politics. Indeed, the very commitment of these groups to democratic pluralism, given their ideologies and their continued armed activities, is questionable.

In some places, domestic agitation and initial American pressure produced substantive gains in political freedom. In Egypt, Yemen, and Morocco, for example, the period immediately following the Iraq war produced tangible results. Egypt held its first-ever competitive presidential ballot, marred though it was by unfair rules, state harassment of opposition candidates, and repression of voters. In Yemen the president committed the government to a new anticorruption drive and allowed a significant degree of competition in his reelection bid. In Morocco a major social reform passed the legislature that vastly improved the legal status of women. The king also accepted the report of a commission investigating state abuses of human rights during the reign of his father. But in each place, progress slowed or even was reversed (notably in Egypt) as American efforts flagged and the executive power reasserted its authority over spheres where greater liberty had temporarily reigned.

Surveying the region in late 2007, one sees the Lebanese government stalemated between allies and adversaries of neighboring Syria, with the militant group Hizballah nearly able to tip the government into irrelevance. The Palestinian Authority, struggling under the weight of Fatah's entrenched corruption and Hamas's violent intransigence, has split into two rival entities in the West Bank and Gaza. In Egypt, major opposition leaders are back in prison and the country holds its breath to see what Mubarak's death might hold in store. It is not a pretty picture, and realists are reasonably tempted to avert their eyes and try to return to the comfort of the old policy framework—one in which dictators did as America wanted, more or less, in exchange for American indulgence of their illiberalisms.

But that comforting framework is no longer available. One way or another, major changes are coming to Middle East governments. The United States can try to prevent those changes, but for reasons I lay out in the following chapters, it is highly unlikely to succeed in the long run and will pay a huge price for the effort to stand behind the region's repressive forces. The alternative is to try to shape the change, to encourage and cultivate those forces and institutions most congenial to Western values and interests. Uniquely at this moment in history, the United States has a crucial role to play in the future of the Middle East. America's overwhelming military and economic dominance of world affairs since the cold war, its brash but irrevocable intervention in Iraq, its indispensable role in Arab-Israeli relations, and its close military relations with many Arab leaders and governments make its attitude toward domestic Arab political development a significant variable in the way these changes play out. America's enduring interests in the Middle East do not allow it to take a neutral stance toward the question of Arab democracy.

In the next chapter I look at the challenges that have historically beset American efforts to promote democracy abroad and that long prevented the United States from making any serious attempts to do so in the Arab world. I explore the two chief impediments—the conflict between democracy promotion and other strategic interests, and the risks of Islamist takeover—that have handicapped even the Bush administration's landmark efforts.

In chapter three I explain the factors that have, until now, largely sustained Arab autocracy even while democratization has transformed every other part of the globe. I also explain why the status quo that the United States has so long defended in the Middle East is no longer viable, examine the dangers of the current period, and argue that America therefore has little choice but to try to aid a peaceful transition to more democratic politics in the region.

I use chapter four to consider alternatives to a policy of democracy promotion in the Arab world and reveal why none of them will suffice to safeguard American interests or to avoid the pitfalls of instability and extremism, as their proponents claim they will. In chapter five I explore and critique the tools of American policy that have so far been directed toward advancing a democratic transformation of the Middle East. The investments made by the Bush administration match neither its soaring rhetoric nor the necessity and urgency of the enterprise at hand. America's policy of Middle East democracy promotion has so far been beset by ambivalence, a consequence of its inability to resolve the enduring challenges outlined in chapter two. Chapter five lays bare the ambiguity afflicting American policy in the Bush administration and explains the failings of Bush's Freedom Agenda.

In chapter six I describe ways to overcome this debilitating ambivalence and build a sustainable policy of democracy promotion in this challenging environment while protecting key American interests. American leverage in the region is significant, but it cannot be exercised without limit or cost. America's desire to advance democratic politics must be tempered by a grounded assessment of the risks of change in the region and how to hedge against them. A practicable strategy must acknowledge these challenges and focus attention on areas of maximum leverage and efficacy. In particular, I argue, the United States must seek in all its efforts to advance basic political freedoms for Arab citizens, which are key to resolving the dilemmas of democratization in this region. The United States must therefore be willing to put other elements of U.S. policy at stake in pressing that end with its Arab allies.

In chapter seven I tackle the challenge of integrating Islamist movements successfully into democratic Arab politics. The United States cannot choose the winners and losers in future Arab democracies, and its attitude toward Islamist movements must become far more attuned to regional realities. I develop a framework in this chapter for making American decisions about which groups to condone, to associate with, or to support in the context of broader democratization. The book concludes with a brief discussion of the necessary bureaucratic elements of an effective policy and how support for robust American democracy promotion can be built and sustained among the institutions of American government and society.

Having decided that "America's vital interests and [its] deepest beliefs are now one," as Bush said in his second inaugural address, does not mean that the two will be congruent in every time and place or that democracy promotion requires no difficult choices along the way.[22] A proper understanding of America's role and its limits is necessary to transform a comfortable and only-when-convenient idealism into a sustainable and effective policy. A hard-headed framework for making unavoidable choices about how and when to press for democratic change is necessary to prevent the freedom strategy from being abandoned as impractical when such choices emerge. Think of this book as a realist's argument for democracy promotion in the Middle East and a guidebook for making the choices that a realistic strategy demands.

CHAPTER TWO

Democracy Promotion in U.S. Foreign Policy

Democracy promotion has always been part of United States foreign policy. While the founding fathers—most famously George Washington, in his farewell address—eschewed foreign adventurism and entanglements, they also viewed the political rights and freedoms for which they fought as universal values and hoped their new nation would serve as a beacon for others who aspired to similar liberty. As Thomas Jefferson wrote on the fiftieth anniversary of America's independence, "May it be to the world what I believe it will be (to some parts sooner, to others later, but finally to all), the Signal of arousing men to burst the chains, under which monkish ignorance and superstition had persuaded."[1] The universalism of America's founding ideals and its role as a beacon for others' struggles for liberty have resonated across the history of American foreign policy. Indeed, scholars such as Tony Smith and John Ikenberry have argued that the advance of global democratic development has been a consistent theme during both Democratic and Republican presidential administrations and that it has helped define America's role in the world: "Honed in the first instances as a means of countering European imperialism and later given even sharper definition in the struggle against fascism and communism, it was no mere talisman but the cutting edge of the United States' rise to world-power status."[2]

America's foreign policy from World War I to the present clearly displays one pattern: whenever the United States has been on the cusp of a major overseas engagement, the promotion of democracy has been a prominent part of the rationale presented by American politicians and embraced by the American public for the necessity of the commitment. For better or for worse, Americans understand their country's role abroad to be closely linked to the spread of democracy.[3]

But although the global advance of democracy has been a consistent theme in the rhetoric of American foreign affairs, the reality of U.S. policy has often diverged from this line. In fact, America's self-appointed mission of promoting democracy abroad has been tempered by other considerations in many places and times. During the cold war, staunch anticommunists, themselves believers in the universalism of the right to liberty, were in practice frequently willing to support "moderate autocrats friendly to American interests" in developing countries. Jeane Kirkpatrick famously called dictators such as General Anastasio Somoza of Nicaragua and Mohamed Reza Pahlavi, the Shah of Iran, "traditional rulers of semi-traditional societies" whose support for America's anticommunist policies had earned them American backing.[4] Thus the United States provided significant military and economic support to Ferdinand Marcos of the Philippines and, until the late 1980s, turned its head from Marcos's embezzlement of government funds and abuses of human rights. The United States government's willingness to overlook concerns about democracy and human rights in the name of anticommunism was also clearly evident in Latin America, where the United States backed right-wing governments (and, where relevant, antigovernment militias) in Guatemala, Argentina, Chile, Nicaragua, and elsewhere. Even when cold war considerations were muted or absent, the United States sometimes sacrificed concerns over basic political freedoms to economic and strategic interests. Two prominent examples are President George H. W. Bush's weak response to China's Tiananmen Square massacre in 1989 and President Bill Clinton's later abandonment of attempts to link trade benefits for China to its human rights record.[5]

In other places and times the United States has spoken out in favor of democracy without pressuring friendly governments to advance it on any particular timetable. This gap between rhetoric and policy generated resentment among indigenous democratic activists living in Taiwan and the Republic of Korea, for example. But when those indigenous movements gained strength, America embraced the trend and supported those countries' democratic transitions. Even in the Philippines, President Reagan eventually withdrew American support for Marcos when the indigenous democratic opposition became too popular and Marcos's repression of it too violent to ignore.

America's mixed record has implanted doubt in many minds about the essential sincerity—and, more pragmatically, the reliability—of America's stated commitment to advancing democracy abroad. Some analysts and activists even reject the idea that the United States is interested in democracy for its own sake, arguing that instances of American support for democratic transformation are properly understood as smokescreens for the pursuit of national interests, mainly economic.[6] Indeed, even some experts who reject the smokescreen argument worry that democracy promotion is a dangerous temptation for American foreign policy, leading the United States into imperialistic behaviors based on a belief in the superiority of its own values and institutions.[7]

In most regions of the globe, America's interest in and support for democratic development has varied considerably. In the Middle East, though, the American record is consistent. In the name of stability and anticommunism, the United States regularly and overtly backed dictators and monarchs, providing diplomatic, military, and economic assistance to bolster these autocrats against enemies both foreign and domestic. Nowhere has the disjuncture between American values and America's foreign policy been as great, as consistent, for as long as in the Arab Middle East.

America's core objective in the Middle East has been—and remains— regional stability. Stability there is necessary to ensure the free flow of oil and gas through the Persian Gulf to world markets, to facilitate the movement of U.S. naval and commercial traffic from the Mediterranean to the Indian Ocean via the Suez Canal, and to protect the security of key regional allies, including the State of Israel and the Kingdom of Saudi Arabia. For six decades America's interest in a stable Middle East was, by and large, well served by its support of status-quo Arab regimes, including most prominently the al-Saud dynasty, Jordan under the late King Hussein and his son King Abdullah II, and, beginning in the 1970s, Egypt under Anwar Sadat and his successor, Hosni Mubarak. The United States helped the young King Hussein of Jordan stabilize his rule in the face of challenges from neighbors and a restive domestic Palestinian population. In the immediate post–World War II years, America was generally regarded as free of the colonial taint of European powers. The United States assisted Saudi Arabia in building its oil industry and modernizing its domestic infrastructure and was rewarded with a Saudi commitment to oil price stability that was broken only once, in the Arab oil embargo that followed the 1973 Arab-Israeli war.[8]

The United States, through adroit diplomacy, a degree of pressure, and extensive military and economic assistance, won Egypt—the Arab world's most populous (and at the time its most politically influential) state—away from the Soviet orbit and eventually brokered Egypt's peace with Israel. The Egyptian-Israeli peace treaty was greased with even more American aid, but it solidified America's dominant position in the region, consolidated Egypt's shift from regional adventurer to regional stabilizer, facilitated the country's hesitant moves toward a market economy, and broke Israel's regional isolation.

Likewise, Washington's support of Saddam Hussein's Iraq during his long war with Iran served America's interest in stability, because Saddam's onslaught prevented the revolutionary Islamism of Khomeini's Iran from extending its influence further into the gulf, a move that would have undermined the stability of Saudi Arabia and other oil-producing states. When Saddam Hussein gassed his own population in the midst of that conflict, America's official response was mild. Only when Hussein turned his revisionist ambitions on American allies Kuwait and Saudi Arabia, threatening global energy supplies, did the United States turn against him.

Although Arab human rights activists can point to a not-insignificant human toll, the relationships the United States built with autocratic Arab leaders during the twentieth century served U.S. interests well, on the whole, and contributed to peace and stability in the region. Any temptation on the part of the United States to consider human rights or democratization in Middle East policy during the period preceding the presidency of George W. Bush was blunted by two fundamental forces that still hold strong sway over U.S. policy today.

The first of these is the belief that more assertive American democracy promotion in the Arab world would inevitably exacerbate tensions with Arab states whose cooperation on other issues is highly valued. Promoting democratic transformation might be cost-free for the United States in Libya or Syria, states whose regimes have been unreliable partners and whose foreign policies have long caused Washington headaches. But the Middle East is full of regimes with which America has worked closely for years and whose cooperation it still desires on a variety of security and economic issues. The potential for conflict between efforts to promote democracy and efforts to achieve other core U.S. strategic goals has been a long-standing obstacle to concerted U.S. pressure for internal political reforms.

This "conflict-of-interests" problem manifests itself in two distinct ways. First, there is the concern, widespread among U.S. policymakers, that putting a greater emphasis on democracy in America's dialogue with Arab regimes will necessarily bump other issues down the priority list or even demand trade-offs. Second, there is the belief that U.S.-Arab cooperation, despite being rooted in mutual self-interest, is fragile and that pressure on Arab governments to yield power at home will lead those governments to loosen or even abandon their strategic alliances with Washington.

Because of these worries, the U.S. government has typically subordinated its concerns about governance and human rights to cold war imperatives and other core issues, such as the Arab-Israeli peace process. Although human rights violations and religious repression in Arab states are regularly noted in the State Department's annual reports on these topics, they have rarely ranked very high on the agenda for face-to-face dialogue between American and Arab officials.

The conflict-of-interests problem has not gone away. Conflicts between democracy promotion and other strategic U.S. goals in the Middle East remain inevitable, given that those other goals rely for the most part on close cooperation with the current slate of Arab governments. Yet the existence of such conflicts does not entirely preclude American efforts to advance political rights and freedoms. Broad consensus exists among America's foreign policy elites that, in the long term, democracy in the Middle East and indeed worldwide will work in America's favor and in the interests of international peace and stability.[9] In the short term, however, conflicts often arise between steps that would advance the pursuit of democracy and other steps that could or should be taken in pursuit of nearer-term objectives. Cooperation in counterterrorism investigations, in regional peacemaking, and in U.S.-Arab trade may favor near-term decisions with tangible benefits at the expense of the long-term, amorphous goal of democratization.

The problem in practice is that promoting a transition to democracy in an autocratic country is always a long-term objective whose progress is difficult to assess. One rarely knows, at a given moment, whether the events one observes in a country's political life will prove to have been a tipping

point in a democratic transition or merely a brief moment of relative freedom in an otherwise unrelieved era of autocracy. Transitions to democracy
are rarely unidirectional, rarely without stalls and reversals.[10] How difficult
it can be, then, to justify sacrificing a clearly identifiable objective in some
arena of material interest in the name of a potential gain for democracy that
can be accurately weighed only in retrospect. Moreover, human rights and
democracy are such perennial concerns that there will always be another
occasion to discuss them. Only rarely does an event such as a rigged election
or a mass protest force America's hand. This increases the temptation by senior officials and line officers alike to push democracy concerns down the priority list and save that necessarily unpleasant conversation for another day.

Considering how frequently America's diplomats must rank-order its
policy priorities in dealing with other countries and how commonly day-to-
day conflicts arise between concrete, short-term objectives and the long-
term pursuit of democracy, it is perhaps remarkable that political freedom
makes it onto the list of U.S.-Arab talking points at all. What rational U.S.
official would sacrifice the pursuit of hard-headed American security or
commercial interests for a mush-headed, ill-defined goal like the advancement of political freedom where none now exists and the prospects for
developing any are slim?

The conflict-of-interests problem also confounds the effective promotion of democracy by the United States in a more insidious, *anticipatory*
way. Policymakers, even at a relatively high level, have come to believe that
certain hard-won types of U.S.-Arab cooperation valuable to the United
States remain precarious and liable to disruption should American pressure
be brought to bear on behalf of democratic progress. Especially with regard
to security cooperation, and even more vociferously since September 11,
2001, experienced American officials and their counterparts in the policy
commentariat warn their colleagues and superiors against pushing too hard
on Arab leaders for greater political openings—for fear that the ax might fall
on some issue dearer to America's heart, or perhaps closer to its jugular.

Most fundamentally, U.S. officials recognize that although democracy in
the long run is good for stability, democratization is often volatile and
uncertain. Indeed, recent studies suggest that countries undergoing democratic transitions are more likely to go to war with a neighbor than either
consolidated democracies or secure autocracies.[11] A real risk exists that a
transition to democracy will itself produce threats to key American interests

or to internal or regional stability in the Middle East. Advocating more democratic practices can also carry direct costs. For example, improving legal due process standards in Arab countries might reduce those countries' abilities to assist in U.S. counterterrorism efforts by carrying out arrests, interrogations, or surveillance that would be impossible under American legal standards.[12]

This preemptive dampening of the democracy promotion flame is most obvious with regard to two long-standing and close American allies, Egypt and Saudi Arabia. Foreign policy experts and career officials alike note that Egyptian cooperation on Arab-Israeli relations is a strategic asset to the U.S. government, one in which previous American administrations invested decades of diplomacy and billions of dollars. But democracy in Egypt might yield a government deeply unfriendly to the United States, perhaps even one that would threaten abrogation of the Camp David accords.[13] These voices also argue that Egypt's cooperation in the Arab-Israeli peace process, among other issues, has always rested on a firm foundation of American support for Egypt's regime. An uncertain campaign for free Egyptian politics, they suggest, will upset this carefully constructed apple cart. If, for example, the U.S. Congress conditioned aid to Egypt on steps toward political reform, they warn, Hosni Mubarak might respond to undue American pressure for democracy by rejecting the nearly $2 billion in annual military assistance he now receives from the Pentagon and turning, as Nasser did, to Russian equipment and training—or perhaps to Chinese.[14]

Similarly, in Saudi Arabia the security cooperation that enabled the United States' forward positioning in the Persian Gulf through the 1990s and up until 2003, and Saudi Arabia's concomitant cooperation on counterterrorism and the containment of Iraq and Iran, came only after many favorable arms deals, an existential threat against Saudi Arabia from Saddam Hussein, and finally a growing jihadist movement led and populated by Saudi citizens who targeted American and Saudi interests. U.S.-Saudi counterterror and security cooperation is viewed in many quarters of the U.S. government as essential for fighting al Qaeda and defending Western interests in the oil-rich gulf region. Iraq's descent into civil conflict only magnifies the importance of Saudi Arabia's stabilizing role in the region. Pressing the al-Saud regime on basic human rights issues, much less on political participation or governmental accountability, is considered by some analysts and policymakers as foolhardy in the extreme. Not only might such unwelcome pressure lead the Saudi royal family to question the wisdom of its strategic alliance with the United States, they argue, but the advent of greater openness in the kingdom might produce instability that could be exploited by local religious extremists or al Qaeda supporters and lead to the takeover of the Arabian peninsula's largest country by radical jihadists.[15]

Fortunately, as I will show, this image of U.S.-Arab relations as delicate, resting on American largesse and easily threatened is profoundly inaccurate as a depiction. Relations between the two countries, over the past sixty years, have rested more than anything on strong foundations of mutual interest.

The second broad problem that haunts American democratization efforts is that this country's general preference for democratic politics has long been tempered, in regard to the Arab world, by the knowledge that the victors of a democratic process in most Arab countries are unlikely to be parties who shared America's policy preferences in the region. Indeed, they might prove actively anti-American and perhaps even antidemocratic once in office.[16] In 1953 the United States and Britain conspired with the Shah of Iran to overthrow a democratically elected, left-leaning prime minister, Mohammed Mossadegh—a betrayal of democratic principles that still carries consequences for U.S.-Iranian relations.[17] Although American policymakers might have begun to regret their actions to constrain Iranian public demands by the time of the 1979 Islamic revolution, the radically ideological tenor of the new regime and its bloody purges of liberal elements from Iranian politics and society seemed only to confirm American prejudices that nothing good could come of popular regime change in the Middle East. Rather, as Jeane Kirkpatrick wrote in 1979: "Hurried efforts to force complex and unfamiliar political practices on societies lacking the requisite political culture, tradition, and social structures not only fail to produce desired outcomes; if they are undertaken at a time when the traditional regime is under attack, they actually facilitate the job of the insurgents."[18] Given this experience in Iran, it was natural for U.S. officials, beginning in the early 1990s, to take a similarly dim view of the prospect of Islamist movements taking the reins in Arab states, even if it were done peacefully.

In the years following the fall of the Berlin Wall, the winds of change in the global environment produced democratic transformations in eastern

Europe, East Asia, and Latin America. The Middle East was not immune from the spirit of this "third wave" of democratization, but neither did it succumb. Algeria's postcolonial, military-led government went farthest in the region along the path toward democracy during this period. Beginning in 1988, Algeria's revolutionary regime began to loosen political controls, and by mid-1991 several major new political parties were preparing to contest the country's first free National Assembly elections. But when the main Islamist party, the Islamic Salvation Front (known by its French acronym, FIS), built on its growing popularity to call a general strike and press for presidential elections, the Algerian president declared a state of emergency. After a first round of parliamentary elections in December 1991 produced an overwhelming FIS victory, the president dissolved parliament altogether and stepped aside in favor of military rule. Over the next ten years Algeria's military and Islamist opposition waged a civil war that killed approximately 120,000 people.[19]

The notion that democracy in the Arab world might yield fundamentalist Islamic regimes instead of liberal pluralism had been a matter of concern in Washington since the Shah's fall in 1979, and the concern was accelerated with the assassination of U.S. ally and peacemaker Anwar Sadat by an Egyptian Islamist in 1981. So when the Algerian election results were tallied and appeared likely to produce the Arab world's first democratically elected theocracy, Washington was primed to oppose the development. The United States, caught up as it was in the dramatic developments in eastern Europe and the Arab-Israeli arena, did not spare a great deal of attention for Algeria's abortive democratic experiment. The U.S. government chose to follow the lead of Algeria's former colonial overlord, France, in its reaction to the military coup of 1992. After an initial expression of concern, the State Department quickly backed away from the issue, with spokeswoman Margaret Tutweiler saying, "We're not going to take sides."[20]

The Algerian experiment and its bloody conclusion have become a prism through which many different actors in the Middle East, and the West, still view the question of Islamist participation in Arab politics. To America and the West, the Algerian experiment was proof that the Iranian Revolution was not an outlier but a premonition of things to come. As one reporter put it at the time, "the success of the Islamic Front indicates that sectarian differences are no barrier to the spread of Muslim fundamentalist politics."[21] The prospect of an FIS victory in Algeria in 1992 slowly crystallized in State Department discourse as the nightmare vision of what democracy might bring to the Arab world: legitimately elected Islamist governments that were anti-American, illiberal, and ultimately antidemocratic. In a speech to the Meridian International Center after the military coup in Algeria, Edward Djerejian, then the assistant secretary of state for Near Eastern Affairs, laid out the resulting attitude toward Islamists and Arab democracy that was to dominate the next decade of U.S. policy: "We are suspect of those who would use the democratic process to come to power, only to destroy that very process in order to retain power and political dominance. While we believe in the principle of 'one person, one vote,' we do not support 'one person, one vote, one time.'"[22] Better to have no elections than elections that produced such an outcome.

But like a prism, the abortive Algerian experiment displays different meanings to different observers. To Arab autocrats, the violence that followed the cancellation of the elections, and the brutality of Islamist terrorism in the years afterward, was proof positive that despite verbal assurances to the contrary, Islamist movements would settle for nothing less than total political victory and would not respect the rule of law or formal political procedures when their outcomes were not to the Islamists' liking. Thus Arab leaders (and secularists as well) often argue that allowing free Islamist participation in politics will send a society over the edge into violent chaos. Arab rulers regularly cite the Algerian example to show why more democracy is dangerous—the Islamists who wish to compete would merely use the opportunity to impose a clerical regime.[23] This argument gained strength with U.S. policymakers in the wake of the 9/11 attacks. A former CIA official noted that "these regimes are not stupid. . . . they raise the Islamist threat and we fall for it, because we want their counterterrorism cooperation. That has trumped the idea of democracy."[24]

To Islamist movements elsewhere in the Arab world, the Algerian experience taught a different lesson: it demonstrated the insincerity of both Arab and Western political leaders' commitment to democratization. When push came to shove, the Algerian leadership showed its willingness to impose military rule rather than accept the legitimate democratic victory of an Islamist party. The lack of protest from Washington demonstrated its hypocrisy in claiming to support democratic transformation. This conclusion—that despite all rhetoric to the contrary the West is unwilling to accept Islamists governing an Arab state—is deeply ingrained among many Islamist leaders today.[25]

American policy since the Algerian coup has evinced a near allergy to official contacts with Islamist movement leaders. This skittishness resulted in part from the harsh experience of the Iranian Revolution, in part from the record of violence among Islamists in Egypt, Lebanon, Algeria, and Gaza in the 1990s, and in part from reasonable suspicions regarding the sincerity of Islamists' professed commitment to democracy and understandable American preferences for liberal and secular parties. In part, too, it stemmed from deference to the preferences of largely secular U.S.-allied regimes that objected to any legitimation of Islamist opposition movements.

Whatever the source, one unfortunate result of the allergic American reaction to Islamist movements in the 1990s was a failure to differentiate, even as the radical Islamist threat to the United States materialized in the late 1990s, among the different types of Islamist groups that were then evolving within Arab societies and among their different attitudes toward Arab political change. Between 1991 and 2001 the world of political Islam diversified significantly, so that today the term *Islamist* can be applied to such a diverse set of groups as to be almost meaningless as a descriptor, encompassing terrorists who flew planes into the World Trade Center along with legislators who voted on behalf of women's suffrage in Kuwait.

And yet, given the prominence of Islamist movements—legal and illegal, violent and peaceful—among the political opposition across the Arab world, the necessity of drawing relevant distinctions and developing a clear and consistent U.S. policy to deal with them is obvious. Ambivalence over how the United States should orient itself toward Islamist movements is one of the key obstacles to developing a credible, effective, and sustainable policy of democracy promotion in the Arab world. The Bush administration's failure to overcome the legacy of Algeria and to develop a more sophisticated relationship with the region's varied Islamist movements severely hampered the effectiveness and indeed the basic credibility of its democracy push. The danger of this failure is evident in the swift backlash against democracy promotion that swept Washington in the wake of several dismaying election results, most notably the victory of Hamas in the Palestinian territories in January 2006 but also the strong showing by Hizballah in the Lebanese elections in 2005 and the Muslim Brotherhood's significant gains in Egyptian elections the same year. As one journalist asked, "How is it possible to promote democracy and fight terrorism when movements deemed by the United States to be terrorist and extremist are the most politically popular in the region?"[26]

To avoid the perceived risks of Islamist takeovers and the perceived costs of prioritizing democracy over other, more immediate goals, the U.S. government's reform efforts in the Arab world before 2001 were generally small, were undertaken in full consultation with the targeted governments, and emphasized technical assistance to government institutions rather than support for nongovernmental social groups. Assistance for "democracy and governance" was (and still is) just a small part of the U.S. Agency for International Development's larger program for the region, which tends to emphasize projects in health care, education, and other core development concerns. Until a few years ago American policy statements occasionally mentioned popular will and human rights, but these issues never intruded on close U.S.-Arab ties. The question of whether they do in 2008, five years after President Bush launched his Freedom Agenda, is still an open one.

The United States, with crucial strategic interests at stake in the Middle East, began in the 1990s to look more closely at the domestic picture in key allies such as Jordan, Egypt, and Saudi Arabia. But the American response to rising regional pressures for change almost never, before September 11, 2001, emphasized democratization as a major element of desirable Arab reforms.[27] Instead, American efforts during the administrations of George H. W. Bush and Bill Clinton focused first on stability in the face of rising Islamist popularity and second on advancing economic liberalization and integration of Arab states into the global economy. These limited efforts at promoting reform were very much afterthoughts in American Middle East diplomacy while two security objectives—resolving the Arab-Israeli conflict and containing Iraq and Iran—took center stage in American policy planning.[28]

In the 1990s America's reform efforts in the Middle East were focused almost exclusively on economic liberalization.[29] The economic reform effort was centered on Egypt and Jordan, key U.S. allies in regional security efforts and in the Arab-Israeli peace process. Jordan won increasing U.S. economic and trade-promotion assistance after it concluded a peace treaty with Israel in 1994, while Egypt and the United States pursued a "Partnership for Economic Growth and Development," also known as the Gore-Mubarak Partnership. According to William Daley, then America's secretary of commerce, the Gore-Mubarak Partnership was designed "to promote economic reform and growth in Egypt and greater U.S.-Egyptian trade."[30] In practice the partnership mainly involved combining pressure from the U.S. government and export-oriented Egyptian businessmen to advance reform in Egypt in the areas of intellectual property protection, commercial law, and credit markets. Political reform was not part of the agenda for discussion. In his annual testimony to Congress on the government's aid request for the Middle East, in June 1996, then assistant secretary of state Robert Pelletreau's discussion of Egypt—America's largest Arab aid recipient at the time—did not mention human rights concerns at all but only the peace process, economic reform, and the Egyptian security services' battle against violent Islamists.[31]

The September 11 attacks shocked the U.S. government into questioning the long-term benefit of its status-quo policy and its relationship to the generation of Islamist terrorism—and also awoke American policymakers to realities in the region that had been growing slowly for a long time and were creating increasing *internal* pressures for change in Arab politics. In response the Bush administration embraced the goal of active democracy promotion in the Middle East as being deeply in American interests, overcoming the United States' long-standing preference for maintaining friendly relations with reliable regional autocrats.

But President Bush found this goal hard to pursue because the two challenges outlined earlier—the problem of competing American interests and the Algeria problem—did not dissipate in the new, post-9/11 environment. If anything, America's new cognizance of its stake in Middle Eastern stability *raised* American sensitivity to the risks inherent in a policy of democratization. Confronting these risks and developing ways to address them are therefore crucial prerequisites for an effective and sustainable policy of democracy promotion in the Middle East—and the Bush administration failed at this essential task.

The difficulty of pursuing a robust democratization program in the Arab world is hardly a surprise. Even at times and in places where the American commitment to promoting democracy has been most sincere and least conflicted, it has been hampered by the fundamental complexity of the enterprise. At its heart, democracy promotion means using the tools of foreign policy in an attempt to influence the domestic politics of another state—always an uncertain enterprise, often ineffectual, and occasionally even counterproductive. Moreover, the programs and projects that the United

States has developed to advance democracy in other countries are fraught with problems: they are often ill designed for their intended operating environment, they apply narrow templates for democratic development, and it is difficult to measure their results and efficacy.[32] Because of these problems, even where America's values and interests are truly and wholly congruent on behalf of democracy promotion, the resulting policies have not always produced positive payoffs and have nearly always been surrounded by controversy both at home and in the target countries.[33]

In the Middle East the United States not only faces the dilemmas of dealing with Islamism, conflicts of interest, and the normal complexity of democracy promotion but also must confront the compounding factor of America's tarnished reputation in the region. The advance of democracy inside a country always rests on the determination of local citizens to participate in government decisionmaking. Throughout the Arab world, as recent headlines and long-running poll results demonstrate abundantly, citizens are interested in greater individual freedom and political participation. But the United States has difficulty tapping into these indigenous pro-democracy sentiments because of widely held and fiercely expressed resentment of the United States and its regional policies, resentment that predates the Iraq war but was exacerbated by it. According to a twenty-one-nation BBC World Service poll in January 2005, 49 percent of Lebanese citizens surveyed said they thought the United States was a "mainly negative" influence in the world. Eighty-two percent of Jordanians and 57 percent of Lebanese did not believe U.S. foreign policy considered others. In another survey only 1 percent of Jordanians and 23 percent of Lebanese respondents said they had "some" or "a lot" of confidence in President Bush "to do the right thing regarding world affairs."[34] Because of this overarching skepticism toward the United States, as well as its inconsistent history on democracy issues, America faces a fundamental credibility gap in speaking to Arab citizens about democracy and thus in forging effective partnerships with regional reformers.

The Pew Global Attitudes Survey in the spring of 2005 found that 80 percent of people in the three Middle Eastern countries in which they surveyed—Lebanon, Jordan, and Morocco—believed that democracy was not a "Western way of doing things" and could work in their country. Another survey, however, found significantly unfavorable views of "American freedom and democracy" among Moroccans, Saudis, Jordanians, Lebanese, and

Emiratis. Even more sobering, a 2006 poll found that 65 percent of Arabs polled in six countries believed that despite the United States' activism on the issue, "democracy is not a real U.S. objective."[35] When the United States is widely resented by Arab citizens, it is difficult to see how America can play a positive role in advancing domestic reforms in Arab countries. Broad public opinion aside, until the United States can build an effective alliance with the Arab world's aspiring democrats, it cannot hope to assist in the project of Arab democratization—but Arab suspicions of U.S. intentions make an alliance difficult to forge.

At the same time, much of the debate in the United States about whether and how to promote democracy in the Middle East centers on a faulty understanding of how democracy promotion relates to U.S. public diplomacy. Some people believe that democracy promotion, to be regarded as successful, must enhance America's popularity among the peoples of the Arab world. Others argue that unless America first repairs its bruised reputation in the region, it cannot hope to affect the growth of democracy in any positive fashion. Neither assertion is necessarily true. Indeed, democracies in the Middle East are, at least at first, unlikely to be as pro-American as some of the United States' autocratic allies have been.[36] It is likely that, as in many other new democracies, popularly elected Arab leaders will burnish their nationalist credentials by railing against the global superpower. But Arab proponents of democracy, like their colleagues in other regions, understand the value of American support for their struggle, even when they would prefer to avoid a tight American embrace. And as in other regions, the United States works for democracy in the Arab world for reasons of long-term national interest, not to win a short-term popularity contest.

These challenges do not add up to the observation that the United States is foolhardy to press for democratic governance in the Arab world. In the long run, building a new social contract between Arab governments and their citizens is necessary for the development of a new equilibrium in Arab regional politics—and for continued fruitful cooperation between Arab governments and the United States on key issues, including stabilizing Iraq, confronting Iran's regional challenge, and promoting Arab-Israeli peace. If Arab governments cannot sustain the support of their citizens, they will be unable to work easily or reliably with the United States on issues of common concern.

In the wake of the Iraq war and the bloody confrontation between Israel and Hizballah in Lebanon in 2006, the relevance of domestic Arab reform to continued U.S.-Arab cooperation is clearer than ever. Hizballah's dynamic leader, Hassan Nasrallah, and Iran's populist president, Mahmoud Ahmadinejad, envision a region defined by unending "resistance" (read: violence, terrorism, and perpetual confrontation) against Israel, the United States, and status-quo Arab governments. Nasrallah and Ahmadinejad argue for the redemptive value of violence and offer the promise of justice and dignity for Arabs humiliated by decades of defeat at the hands of the West and Israel.

The radical vision for the Middle East presented by Iran and its militant allies Hizballah and Hamas is gaining traction in Arab society. Even on the streets of their own cities the leaders of Egypt and Jordan are less popular than Nasrallah and Ahmadinejad; in one poll Hassan Nasrallah was the most popular world leader among Arabs in six states.[37] The radicals' message of resistance is always combined with denunciations of Sunni Arab leaders for cowering under an American security umbrella and making humiliating deals with Israel.

Arab leaders feel keenly the threats from radical Islam within their own societies. They know that Islamists have capitalized on state failures and weaknesses and that the critique put forward by local Islamists is underscored by the resistance rhetoric peddled by Iran and its allies. In this insecure environment, Arab rulers face a dilemma: they know regional stability and their own strategic interests require them to cooperate with the United States, yet America's regional role is intensely unpopular with their publics. Enhancing Arab cooperation with American regional diplomacy would likely require Arab rulers to employ greater repression at home, reinforcing the claims of domestic opponents. To extract Arab rulers from this dilemma and effectively counter the region's radical axis, U.S.-Arab cooperation must rest on a new foundation of partnership among the United States, moderate Arab governments, and their mostly moderate citizens—a partnership designed to produce a better future for the people of the Middle East.

The risks of a concerted pro-democracy effort by the United States in the Arab world are real. But to assess them accurately, one must weigh them against the risks of remaining indifferent. The Middle East has changed in the years since America backed the Kuwaiti and Saudi monarchs against the Iraqi dictator. It has changed in ways that make further shifts in Arab politics likely yet leave the outcome of that change both uncertain and dangerous. In the next chapter I examine this new reality and what it portends.

CHAPTER THREE

The Vanishing
Status Quo

I N A 2005 interview with Jeffrey Goldberg of the *New Yorker,* former
national security advisor Brent Scowcroft argued that protecting the
political status quo in the Arab world had been and remained the correct
policy for the United States. According to Scowcroft, the status quo in the
Middle East had bought the United States "fifty years of peace."[1] Residents of
the Middle East might quarrel with that characterization, for the years after
1948 witnessed five Arab-Israeli wars, wars or major civil conflicts in Yemen,
Algeria, Jordan, and Lebanon, and a war between Iraq and its Persian neighbor, Iran. But Scowcroft's statement reflects the judgment that, from the perspective of American interests, the latter half of the twentieth century went
very well in the Middle East. Despite its upheavals, the region remained
mostly friendly and accommodating to core American interests in energy
stability, maritime access, and the containment of communism.

Among the status-quo rulers on whom the United States relied to preserve these interests were Morocco's King Hassan II, Jordan's King Hussein,
Egypt's Anwar Sadat and Hosni Mubarak, and the succession of sons of
Saudi Arabia's Abdel Aziz al Saud. During the cold war years these rulers
checked the penetration of Soviet influence in the region and contained the
activities of pro-Soviet regional actors. They largely agreed with the United
States on major issues such as the need for stable oil production, the desir-
ability of Arab-Israeli peace, and the need to contain ambitious regional
actors who might undertake local adventures. Throughout the second half

of the twentieth century, superpower rivalries, Arab-Israeli wars, and regional adventurism were the main threats to regional stability.

Today the primary threat to regional stability emanates not from such interstate conflicts but from internal factors. A combination of demographic change, economic stagnation, and political alienation in Arab societies poses a powerful and increasing challenge to the legitimacy of key Arab governments and to their ability to govern peacefully.

A perfect storm is uniting local factors such as population growth and internal corruption with external factors such as the globalization of capital markets and information flows to produce an undeniable challenge to the stability and viability of today's status-quo Arab regimes. An imbalance between demographics, economics, and government capacity is producing a generation of frustrated, urbanized young people with decent educations but few available jobs in their chosen fields and few prospects for marriage or other means of social advancement. This imbalance, combined with the effects of new technologies and globalization in media and culture, is also slowly breaking down the basic social contract—the bargain between citizens and state—that has long sustained America's Arab partners.

Arab states have faced severe economic and political challenges before and emerged intact. Indeed, their ability to survive such domestic pressures has led some analysts to declare that radical regime change in the Arab world is a near impossibility.[2] Whatever the challenge, these analysts argue, Arab rulers are flexible and resourceful enough to escape the noose. As Gregory Gause noted, "the greater the control a state can exercise over society—through coercion, inducement, vesting interests, and the manipulation of symbols and ideologies to gain citizen loyalty—the harder it is going to be for even attractive ideological movements from the outside to find enough local support to threaten the existing order."[3] Indeed, for many years a powerful combination of ideology, money, and effective domestic security forces has lengthened the life spans in office of some Arab rulers who otherwise might long ago have found themselves in the dustbin of history.

This trio of tools—rent, rhetoric, and repression—has kept Arab rulers in power for more than half a century. But the magical trio's effectiveness is breaking down, and escape valves for social pressure, such as outmigration, are increasingly constrained in a post-9/11 world. As the pressure builds, nervous Arab regimes are experimenting with political, social, and economic reforms that will ease the building pressures for change without requiring a real devolution of power. But the interdependent web of social, economic, and political relations that Arab autocrats built to sustain themselves leaves them today without the flexibility they need to deal with these new pressures and still survive in power unscathed. In short, the political status quo in the region—the status quo on which America has long relied to protect its interests—has become unsustainable, and the coming years will see major changes in Arab politics. Undoubtedly some long-time Arab regimes will survive the coming storm, but they will not survive it unchanged. The key question is not whether the regimes will survive but in what form and at what cost to themselves, to their citizens, and to U.S. interests.

Change does not mean, necessarily, democracy. Indeed, less progressive and more destabilizing options for Middle East political and social development are easy to imagine and perhaps more likely than democratization. Arab politics may move along any number of paths in the coming years, but generally speaking, the available paths *other* than increasingly liberal and democratic development are paths fraught with unpalatably high costs for the United States and the region. Among other risks, the likelihood of Islamist takeovers (of an especially unfriendly nature) in the region is far higher in the absence of democratic development than in a more democratic context, a prospect I discuss in chapter seven.

If the future of the Middle East is to be more stable and prosperous than the present, and at least as congenial to American interests as the past, then the inevitable process of change in the Middle East must be managed—mainly by local actors, but with outside assistance—toward a progressive end. The stakes for the United States and the world demand that outside forces, for the first time in the region's modern history, put their thumbs firmly on the scale on the side of Arab democracy.

In the early twentieth century all of today's Arab countries were governed, directly or indirectly, by colonial masters. The Ottoman Empire controlled most of what is now the Arab world until that empire collapsed in 1918. The victorious Allied powers arranged borders and governments for the nation-states that emerged from Ottoman rule. In parts of North Africa and the Persian Gulf, the colonial era persisted into the 1960s. Many scholars have noted the resulting artificiality of nation-state identity in these new countries and the legitimacy problems it created for successive Arab state governments.[4]

Nonetheless, with a few notable exceptions such as Algeria, Arab societies did not have to wage military campaigns to win their sovereign independence; it was granted by the European powers under circumstances that allowed those powers to retain significant economic, military, and political relationships with the successor governments. Moreover, although monarchies were created in most of the successor states, in Iraq and Egypt the monarchs ruled alongside elected parliaments and prime ministers. Indigenous nationalist parties in both these states capitalized on the relatively liberal climate to demand increased independence from Britain and increased concessions from their monarchs to the parliamentary body. And in both countries the parliamentary monarchies were ultimately overthrown in revolutions that brought nationalist forces to power, shut down the democratic processes as they had existed, and replaced them with military-led authoritarian states.

The relatively democratic climate that prevailed after independence in the larger Arab states and their relatively peaceful paths to independence (certainly in comparison with India, Southeast Asia, and much of Africa) have led some intellectuals and activists to hark back to the experience of the 1920s and 1930s as evidence of a "liberal legacy" in Arab politics that could and should now be revived. The Egyptian dissident Saad Eddin Ibrahim, writing shortly after his release from prison in 2003, argued that the liberal age of Islam that was silenced after World War II when authoritarian regimes came to power across the region must be revived: "We saw ourselves not as builders from scratch, but as revivers of a great (but not perfect) tradition that had existed not only in our country but also in Syria, Iraq, Iran, Morocco, and elsewhere. We were and we remain determined that this liberal tradition . . . will not be forgotten."[5]

It is therefore worth recalling that colonialism permeated this era's Arab politics. The major nationalist parties of the early twentieth century arose in the context of continued colonial domination (however direct or indirect in different places) and were dominated by elites educated in Western schools and imbued with Western sensibilities. The historian Albert Hourani noted that early nationalist movements such as the Young Tunisians and Young Algerians were perhaps more concerned with achieving modernization and development, through their continued relationship with the colonial power, than with political independence itself.[6] Thus he wrote:

Power in the newly independent states came in the first instance into the hands of ruling families or educated elites who had the social position and political skill which had been needed during the period of transfer of power. Such groups did not on the whole, however, possess the skill and appeal needed to mobilize popular support in the new circumstances of independence, or to create a state in the full sense. They did not speak the same political language as those whom they claimed to represent, and their interests lay in the preservation of the existing social fabric and distribution of wealth, rather than in changes in the direction of greater social justice.[7]

The so-called liberal era of Arab politics was thus tainted by association with colonial domination, and those liberal nationalist parties that survive today, such as the Egyptian Wafd, are tainted, too, by this history.

Because most Arabs tasted full political independence only during the past sixty years, it is unsurprising that sovereignty, especially with respect to European and Western powers and their policy preferences, remains a key concern in Arab politics. Arab leaders continue to invoke sovereignty as a national priority that serves to legitimate their continued rule and label democratic opposition movements as fifth columns, inspired or supported by the Western powers.

Of course, this emphasis on sovereignty also serves Arab rulers well when they reject Western governments' pressure for improved human rights or democratic freedoms as unwelcome interference in their indigenous political development. Thus the son of Egypt's dictatorial president, who holds no government leadership post himself yet aspires to succeed his father, can still argue against U.S. democracy-promotion efforts, saying, "We reject these foreign ambitions to erase Arab identity in the framework of what they call the Greater Middle East initiative."[8] But over time the cry for enhanced sovereignty has been taken up by opposition movements in Arab states whose leaders are closely aligned with the United States. The very foundation of U.S.-Arab cooperation is vulnerable to appeals on the basis of this political history.

By mid-century, postcolonial Arab nationalism had taken on a revolutionary cast. In the 1950s and 1960s, noted the historian William Polk, "coups were attempted in virtually all the Arab lands."[9] Beginning with the Free Officers' Coup in Egypt in 1952, which quickly brought Gamal Abdel

Nasser to power, many Arab states were overtaken by revolutionary leaders. Nasser was followed by the overthrow of the parliamentary government in Baghdad (1958) and the ascendance of the Baath Party in Damascus (1963). In Sudan, Iraq, Syria, Egypt, and Libya, nationalists succeeded in establishing military-led authoritarian regimes. With the success of anticolonial struggles in Tunisia (1956) and Algeria (1962), nearly every government in the region was espousing one or another version of Arab nationalism.

Arab nationalist ideology merged the rich history of Arab literary, cultural, and political dominance of the Middle East and North Africa with a folkist nationalism in the style of 1920s Germany and the rhetoric of anti-imperialism common at that time across the third world. The result was a pan-Arab political identity that papered over very real sectarian, ethnic, and class distinctions within Arab societies and prioritized the social unity of Arabic-speaking citizens against the external (Western, colonial) enemy over any domestic agenda. The ruling regime, as the vehicle for national realization (in principle through eventual unification of the Arab nation in a single political entity), was owed loyalty by every citizen. In many of the larger Arab states, Arab nationalism was combined with a state-socialist economy that institutionalized and reinforced traditional modes of patriarchal state-society relations, making the government the source and distributor of almost all social goods and thereby marginalizing and suppressing social organizations independent of the state.

Although united in their opposition to Israel and their insistence on national independence vis-à-vis the Western powers, Arab states were not immune to intraregional rivalries—witness the Egyptian-Saudi proxy war in Yemen.[10] At times these rivalries, particularly those between Syria, Egypt, and Iraq, were expressed in terms of which Arab nationalist regime was doing more to advance pan-Arab unity or the war against Israel. Arab nationalism never fully overcame more local forms of political identity—the Egyptian-Syrian condominium, the United Arab Republic, failed after only three years—and indeed sometimes it merged with them. But it did serve as a powerful legitimator for revolutionary and postcolonial regimes that might otherwise have had difficulty sustaining public loyalty or justifying the repression of domestic opponents. Repeated wars with Israel in 1956, 1967, and 1973 and Israel's invasion of Lebanon in 1982 reinforced the legitimation of Arab regimes through their defense of the Arab homeland and their struggle for Arab rights to historic Palestine. Meanwhile, Arab kings and presidents alike consolidated their domestic rule into a well-known form of autocracy that political scientists call corporatist authoritarianism.[11]

The apparently inhospitable environment for democratic development in the Arab world led some to conclude, with Samuel Huntington, that "Western ideas of individualism, liberalism, constitutionalism, human rights, equality, liberty, the rule of law, democracy, free markets, [and] the separation of church and state often have little resonance" in Muslim communities and that "deeply ingrained Islamic" cultural traditions are a "negative condition" that "may prevent democratic development."[12] Such claims echo similar assertions made about other cultures in earlier eras; at various times, Catholic Latin America and Buddhist Japan were both considered culturally deaf to democratic ideas.[13] That consolidated democracies can now be found on every continent of the globe suggests that although culture may shape democratic development, it does not determine it. Self-serving autocratic leaders also sometimes argue that their local culture is ill suited or at least not yet prepared for democratic governance. King Fahd of Saudi Arabia, for example, claimed that "the democratic system prevalent in the world is not appropriate in this region. The election system has no place in the Islamic creed, which calls for a government of advice and consultation and for the shepherd's openness to his flock, and holds the ruler fully responsible before his people." His arguments echo the "Asian values" thesis advanced by Singapore's former dictator, Lee Kuan Yew, to explain why international human rights norms should not be enforced in East Asian nations.[14]

History, however, has proven such arguments ill founded. A majority of the world's Muslims already live in democratic states, including two states with large populations of Muslims, India and Indonesia. And the very existence of democratic movements in many Arab countries is clear witness to the fact that Arab citizens are not, simply by virtue of their cultural or religious identity, immune to the aspiration to self-rule.

The factors that have so far prevented the establishment of a single viable Arab democracy cannot be reduced to culture or religion. In fact, the persistence of Arab authoritarianism stems from multiple, interactive forces, and it has proven correspondingly difficult to erode. The success of Arab regimes at overcoming inhospitable conditions and deflecting manifold challenges to their rule over the past six decades has led some observers to conclude that the regimes are so deeply entrenched as to be indestructible.

Their ideological flexibility, material resources, and willingness to employ force to suppress dissent have made them, these observers judge, experts at muddling through, who can effectively deflect any internal or external attempt to unseat them.[15] Yet the environment that enabled Arab autocrats to build and sustain their regimes has changed in significant ways in the past decade or so, with concomitant challenges for governance.

The Three Rs behind the Durability of Arab Autocrats

The factors that historically have enabled Arab authoritarianism can be summarized as a triad of external income, or "rents," state repression, and effective nationalist rhetoric. I examine each of these "three Rs" in turn.

One of the most powerful and well-understood forces underlying Arab authoritarianism is economic. Many, though not all, Arab states can maintain authoritarian political structures, scholars note, for the simple reason that they do not rely for state income on taxation of the citizenry. As Lisa Anderson observed, "historically, states have become beholden to their citizens through reciprocal obligation" wherein the state's demand for taxes is "soon followed by demands, particularly among property holders, for protection against such arbitrary exactions and for a role in deciding how state income was spent."[16] This traditional linkage between taxation and the demand for representation, which helped inspire the American Revolution, breaks down in the Arab Middle East, where oil resources, nationalization of foreign industries, and foreign aid have all been sources of revenue that were not reliant on citizen compliance. Moreover, Anderson says, these Arab regimes "use their externally generated income to buy acquiescence in their rule" by providing social services and public goods. This externally subsidized welfare statism facilitated, in the eyes of scholars who focus on the "rentier state," the sustenance and persistence of a traditionally paternalistic relationship between Arab state and society.[17]

Between 1970 and 2004, Saudi national income from oil exports totaled $1.6 trillion.[18] Saudi Arabia's windfall oil profits in the 1970s funded a massive expansion of the welfare state, with health care and education guaranteed by the government and with sizable subsidies for housing, utilities, food, and other necessities. Government employment also became widely available to citizens, and the government facilitated the importation of workers for menial and service jobs. In such an environment, private voluntary organizations were superfluous and indeed only called into question the adequacy of the royal family's benevolence. With social welfare guaranteed by the state, what purpose could be served by the existence of interest groups lobbying for citizens' rights? Until a few years ago the only non-governmental organizations legally recognized by the Kingdom of Saudi Arabia were the chamber of commerce and the journalists' syndicate. The kingdom provides a paradigmatic example of how external rents enable the paternalistic authoritarianism of Arab regimes.[19]

Of the Arab states without large oil resources, scholars note, some have managed instead to acquire external "rents" from foreign assistance provided through an alliance with one of the superpowers. Beginning in the early 1950s the Egyptian regime of Gamal Abdel Nasser played the two superpowers against one another in an attempt to extract resources Nasser could use to sustain his revolutionary regime. His alliance with the Soviets was cemented in 1955 with a significant arms deal (via Czechoslovakia) and, a few years later, Soviet financing for the Aswan High Dam. His successor, Anwar Sadat, likewise played the superpower rivalry to his advantage, both economically and diplomatically. He used his ousting of Soviet advisors to win American aid, which smoothed the way for domestic economic reforms and the peaceful reacquisition of the Sinai Peninsula from Israel after three unsuccessful wars. Today, despite Egypt's peace treaty with Israel and the end of the cold war, American assistance to Egypt is mainly military and includes a license to assemble M1A1 "Abrams" tanks in Egypt and subsidies for annual joint military exercises in the Mediterranean, reinforcing Egypt's strategic dominance over all its Arab neighbors.[20] Egypt also garnered access to significant non-tax income by nationalizing the Suez Canal in 1956.

Especially in the oil-rich states, the easy availability to governments of non-tax income enabled the establishment of a paternalistic state-society contract that reinforced traditional Arab patriarchal social relations (and in some places enhanced them with state socialism) and effectively choked off the development of independent power centers in civil society. Easy rents similarly made it easy for Arab governments to buy off dissent and centralize authority by making government the primary organizer of social and economic as well as political life.

Gregory Gause has shown how the governments of Saudi Arabia and other oil-rich states used their income from oil resources to build a network of citizen dependence on and allegiance to the state that effectively insulated these countries from potential sources of instability for many years. The availability and use of oil rents, Gause argued, explained the relative stability of Arab gulf states in the face of the Iranian Revolution in 1979 and efforts by its leader, Ayatollah Ruhollah Khomeini, to foment unrest among Arab Shiites across the gulf.[21]

Easy income from oil and strategic rents, the prevailing climate of superpower competition, and the ongoing Arab-Israeli conflict all facilitated the growth of sizable military establishments and large security services in Arab states, enabling the second leg of our authoritarian triangle, state repression. Military and security forces, financed through external rents, served as important arenas for domestic employment and socialization of young people, tying citizens ever more tightly to government-provided sustenance. And governments have not always resisted the temptation to deploy their large militaries in foreign adventures, which coincidentally provided them a further excuse, in the form of a national security threat, to ignore or suppress domestic dissent. The ongoing conflict with Israel justified massive defense spending, especially in the "ring" states around the Jewish state's borders, but more distant governments in the gulf and the Maghreb also used it to rationalize such expenses. Arab states spent an average of 5.2 percent of their GDP on military expenditures in 2004, versus a world average of 2.5 percent.[22]

These sizable security forces have enabled regimes to be vigorous in their defense of the political status quo and proactive in their suppression of dissenters. Arab regimes have effectively used their military and security forces to intimidate, disrupt, and repress domestic opposition forces on both the right and the left. They have employed emergency laws and other security tools to suppress the formation of independent social forces that could potentially counterbalance state power. In 1979, when demonstrations swept Shiite communities in the Saudi kingdom's oil-producing east, security services swiftly put down the disturbance. The government was able to justify its harsh response by reference to a security threat earlier in the year when a group of zealous (Sunni) religious dissidents took over the Grand Mosque in Mecca. In the secular nationalist states, the dominance of Arab nationalism justified a role for domestic intelligence and security services in monitoring, intimidating, and shuttering organizations espousing contrary views, including not only communist and Islamist opposition movements but also those representing ethnic or religious minorities such as Kurds, Berbers, and Copts. Egypt's Interior Ministry forces, composed of young men with few other job prospects, are present at every political protest in Cairo, often outnumbering demonstrators several times over.

Rents and repression have been the "carrot" and the "stick" coaxing Arab citizens into acquiescence to rule by governments that provided many goods apart from political participation or civil liberties. The third leg of this authoritarian triangle is ideology. Arab regimes have wielded legitimating ideologies, most notably Arab nationalism, to sustain themselves in power. Because of its emphasis on external challenges such as Western colonialism and the perceived colonial imposition of Israel on the Arab region, Arab nationalism heightened and sustained local perceptions of threats and so justified autocratic politics and diverted attention from internal problems. An anonymous Arab author in 2002 wrote:

> I would like to ask [some] questions that have been bothering me since the demonstrations [in solidarity with the Palestinians] that marched through the streets of Arab countries—which brought to mind the demonstrations flooding the streets to defend the honor of the [Arab] nation, as they believed was personified by comrade Saddam [in 1990 during the gulf crisis.] Is there even one Arab country in which these demonstrations were spontaneous? . . . I ask: Why don't these officials hasten to protest the terrible state (indeed the absence) of basic services in their countries, which have no health, education, or [social] services. . . . They are all preoccupied with Palestine, and with the slogan "No voice is higher than the voice of battle."[23]

In the ideological context of Arab nationalism that makes this slogan ubiquitous, those raising criticisms of the ruler or his policies can quickly be labeled disloyal to the national cause. In the name of national unity against external threat, dissent and even discussion of internal difficulties can be stifled and violently repressed.

Easy rents, state repression, and Arab nationalist rhetoric worked well because they worked in tandem, reinforcing one another in ways I have mentioned. In the past, governments used state largesse to bind citizens to the government and to co-opt opposition elements and make them complicit in the status quo. Remaining dissent was delegitimated by governing ideologies and repressed by state security forces.

Today, however, rents, repression, and rhetoric are less readily available, more difficult to employ, and less effective than in the past. Domestic pressures—notably demographic changes—have combined with changes in international politics and society to pose challenges to Arab autocratic governments that are difficult for them to overcome without a wholesale renovation of the social contract between rulers and ruled. External rents from superpowers have dried up significantly since the end of the cold war, and oil rents, even in an era of high crude prices, cannot keep pace with the astonishing population growth the region has experienced and the pressures a young population places on social services and labor markets. The Arab regimes also face a much narrower range for repressive action before incurring unacceptable political costs. The ideology of Arab nationalism has lost its force as a legitimator for regimes, and global forces have altered the expectations citizens, especially young citizens, have of their government. As a result of these domestic and international changes, the social contract that previously lay at the heart of Arab government stability is frayed, and the stability and legitimacy of today's Arab regimes rest on a knife's edge.

Challenges to Arab Authoritarianism

Although rentierism has been a bulwark of Arab authoritarianism, its logic is beginning to fail as the relationship between incoming rents and domestic demands falls out of balance. Demographically the Middle East has experienced an unprecedented baby boom over the past twenty years, one that makes America's post–World War II baby boom look like a mere blip.[24] This population growth, and its skewed age distribution, is slowing, but not abruptly. Today, 37.1 percent of the Arab world population is under 15 (figure 3-1).[25] The large cohort of younger adults who are of child-bearing age means that even if family size shrinks, the "youth bulge"—the large proportion of young people in the total population—in the Arab world will remain for years to come.

The disproportionate number of young people in today's Arab world "can be either a demographic gift or a demographic curse," noted the United Nations Development Program in 2005, "depending on whether countries can use the human potential represented by their populations well enough to satisfy people's aspirations for a fulfilling life."[26] In other words, young people can be a source of strength and growth in a society if their basic needs are provided for, if they are given a decent foundation of education and health, and if they can be successfully integrated into adult society

Figure 3-1. *Population and Age Structure in Selected Arab States, 2000 and 2025*

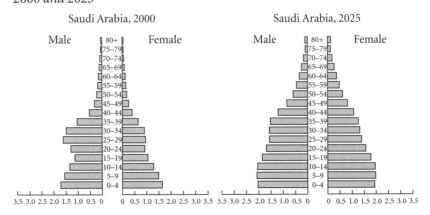

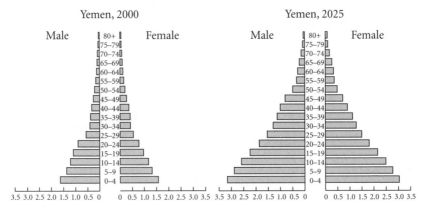

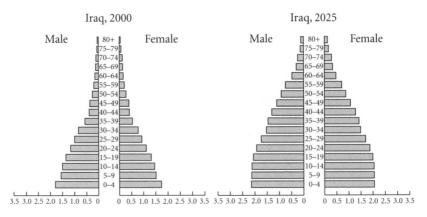

Source: U.S. Bureau of the Census, International Database, Population Pyramids (www.census.gov/ipc/www/idb/).

through employment, marriage, and family formation. But meeting these requirements for a large young population places tremendous demands on government and society.

The growing population of young adults in the Arab world is a problem for regional stability because, as Graham Fuller noted in 2003, "the requisite conditions that could beneficially absorb and gainfully employ a growing population are simply not present."[27] The most urgent imbalance is in employment. As the current cohort of Arab youth enters the job market over the next two decades, it will demand a total of 80 million new jobs. This demand for new jobs is exacerbated by existing unemployment rates in the region, which average 10 to 15 percent and in some countries reach nearly 30 percent.[28]

Economists estimate that in the next twenty years the Arab states together will have to double their current employed labor force to accommodate these new workers and slowly absorb existing unemployment. This amounts to a total of 100 million new jobs, or, in the words of a noted economist, "creating as many jobs in the next 15 years as was done in the last five decades."[29]

In the past, Arab economies dealt with excess labor supply through two main routes: public sector employment and international migration. Neither route can suffice to absorb the young people coming into the labor market over the next two decades.[30] The public sector in most Arab states is already bloated, because government employment was a key means of co-optation in earlier times, and many governments promised (some continue to promise) a civil service job to every university graduate. State employment is a virtual sinecure in many places and includes retirement and other benefits unavailable elsewhere—making it an expensive labor-absorption program for already cash-strapped governments. In the past two decades the demands of the global economy have created pressures to shrink the state sector and its role in the overall economy. Especially now that governments have begun to divest themselves of previously state-owned industries, they offer fewer and fewer productive jobs. Legions of civil servants have little to do. International migration is also increasingly unavailable as a way of reducing local unemployment. The more populous Arab states of North Africa and the Levant used to send their sons to the gulf states to work, but those states are now reducing their migrant workforces in order to reserve more local jobs for their own citizens.[31] And outlets for immigration to Europe and the United States are increasingly stymied, both by much tighter border security since September 11, 2001, and by Western publics' increasing rejection of expanded immigrant labor.

If the government sector in Arab states is shrinking, and migration cannot absorb enough job seekers, then the only other solution is to create more private sector jobs. The Arab private sector has rebounded from the height of Arab socialism in the 1960s, but it cannot yet create sufficient jobs to pick up the slack in the labor market. The pace of economic reform and the quality of the business environment in the Arab countries have been insufficient to induce either Arab or Western investors to build the region's private sector in a way that would produce large numbers of new jobs. In the gulf countries, legal frameworks and market incentives still encourage private businesses to import cheap labor from South Asia instead of hiring locals. Many gulf states have enacted laws to compel businesses to hire native citizens rather than guest workers, but studies show that young Arab university graduates prefer to remain unemployed or work in the "informal sector"—that is, drive taxis or run unregistered small businesses such as food carts—sometimes for years, in the hope of eventually securing a civil service job.[32] Furthermore, many Arab young adults, even university graduates, lack the job skills and productivity levels that the private sector is seeking. This mismatch between Arab educational output and the private sector's needed inputs contributes to a situation that frustrates the employment prospects of a generation of Arab youth.[33]

One might expect that for some states, at least, oil wealth in an era of rising prices would provide sufficient resources to manage this demographic boom. A rentier state selling $80-a-barrel oil might be able to absorb new workers through massive state infrastructure projects that create jobs or even through an unnecessary expansion of the bureaucratic payroll in government ministries. But the centralization of power and wealth, developed over years by governments that used national income to co-opt any substantial alternative power center, prevents such solutions from taking hold. Instead of being used to spread wealth and meet citizens' needs, binding them once again to the state, rising oil rents are benefiting the few. As oil income and economic growth rise, income inequality is skyrocketing (figure 3-2).

The economic pressures created by mounting youth unemployment might be addressable through rapid economic growth if new investment in industrial and other productive enterprises could create new jobs. Some Arab states, in bids to win more foreign direct investment, have worked to

Figure 3-2. *GDP Growth and Income Inequality in the Arab World,*
1975–99

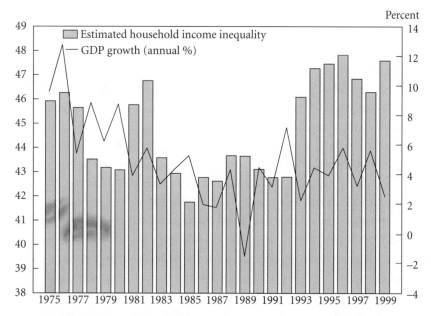

Source: Steven Heydemann, "Upgrading Authoritarianism in the Arab World," Saban
Center Analysis Paper 13 (Brookings, October 2007).

improve their business environments by making the structural economic
reforms and other changes that make up the "Washington consensus." But
these reforms include steps, such as selling off state-owned industries, cutting government subsidies on basic goods, and floating the national currency, that further reduce the state's influence over society, often provoke
hardship, and can thus catalyze precisely the kinds of social instability that
Arab regimes are trying to prevent. Furthermore, the networks of corrupt
relations between governments and private sector elites that help sustain
Arab authoritarianism make structural liberalization difficult for regimes to
implement.[34] When governments privatize state industries or increase competition and transparency in government contracting, they often threaten
the interests of business elites who have long traded comfortable contracts
or kickbacks for political support of the regime. The recent history of the
Middle East features several states that have embarked on the path of structural reform but balked in the face of mass protests against dislocation or
protests from key elites.

There remains a significant difference, of course, between economic and political pressures on Arab regimes and political instability. In earlier periods of economic insufficiency, when young people were swayed by larger social trends, analysts confidently predicted political upheaval for Arab states—yet the regimes survived. Throughout the 1980s, when oil prices were in relative decline, analysts warned that disenchanted, urbanized youths, inspired by the Islamic revolution in Iran, would shake the foundations of Arab governments. Islamist movements in the region generated mass mobilizations against some regimes and organized terrorism against others. Yet the regimes managed, through a combination of co-optation and repression, to survive this previous period of challenge. Why, then, does today's reality appear to present a more significant challenge to Arab authoritarianism and a greater risk of regional instability?

In the past, Arab regimes survived these challenges in part because they were able to expand the state in ways that brought benefits to a larger proportion of the population and made the state the source of most social and economic goods in society. State employment, educational benefits, and other social goods were used to make citizens reliant on state largesse and thus less likely to express dissent. But the Arab state is shrinking not only in terms of its ability to employ large numbers of people but also in its broader capacity to bind citizens to the government through penetration of the economy and by acting as the primary source of social goods. In the early 1990s, Arab state capacity was prodigious and served well to buy citizens' loyalty and suppress dissent. Today the situation is quite different. Tables 3-1 and 3-2 reveal a downward trend in state capacity in major Arab countries, as measured by the state's share of the economy and by the proportion of the population serving in the armed forces. These two measures indicate how well the state can penetrate society by providing resources and accessing societal labor.

As Gause noted in 1991, oil and other rents enabled "material links between citizens and the state apparatus," thereby encouraging loyalty—but tight links to the state also encouraged people to "make more political demands on the regime, including demands for political participation."[35] In recent years, Arab state capacity has been shrinking rather than growing while the youth bulge and access to global information flows have ratcheted up social demands.

Table 3-1. *Government Spending as Percentage of GDP,*
Selected Countries, 1975–2005

Year	Egypt	Jordan	Kuwait	Saudi Arabia	Syria
1975	24.9	34.7	11.1	14.6	21.1
1980	15.7	28.8	11.2	15.9	23.2
1985	17.2	26.3	22.4	31.9	23.8
1990	11.3	24.9	38.7	29.2	14.3
1995	10.5	17.1	32.2	23.6	13.4
2000	11.2	17.0	21.5	26.0	12.4
2005	12.8	15.3	15.4	23.1	13.5

Source: World Bank Development Indicators, 2007. Data for Jordan were unavailable for 1975, so the figure for 1976 was used.

The days of easy rents with which Arab regimes could win citizen loyalty and buy off dissent are now over. Although oil-rich states may be enjoying soft budget constraints at the moment, this will likely be insufficient to overcome long-standing structural imbalances or integrate huge young populations into existing social structures. But the next tool for sustaining Arab authoritarianism, repression, is also less available to Arab states than it once was. The domestic repression once used by many Arab regimes to contain organized opposition forces is now far more visible to the public both at home and internationally. International media and pan-Arab satellite channels are one factor in this visibility. When Egyptian security forces beat up demonstrators in 2005 during a controversy over amending the

Table 3-2. *Number of Members of the Armed Forces per*
Thousand Population, Selected Countries, 1975–2005[a]

Year	Egypt	Iraq	Israel	Jordan	Saudi Arabia	Syria
1975	8.6	12.2	119.0	29.4	5.3	24.1
1985	9.2	34.7	119.1	26.5	7.8	36.6
1995	7.6	18.2	107.0	22.4	8.2	29.6
2005	6.0	6.9	91.8	17.4	10.3	16.7

Sources: "The Military Balance," 1975–76, 1985–86, 1995–96, 2005–06 (London: International Institute for Strategic Studies).

a. Figures for Israel include both active and reserve forces. Figures for Saudi Arabia in 1975 and 1985 are based on the lowest listed estimated total populations. Figures for Saudi Arabia in 1995 and 2005 are based on the number of Saudi nationals in the total population.

constitution, state television ignored the story, but Al Jazeera did not, and the government's brutality to peaceful demonstrators was seen throughout the country, the region, and the world. Human rights monitoring groups now use the Internet to mobilize global public relations campaigns on a few hours' notice. And increasingly, local webloggers in Arabic, English, and French keep the world informed of the steps Arab governments take to stifle internal dissent.

In this information-rich environment, human rights violations are poorly tolerated internationally, even by allies who value the stability such measures once ensured. Since 1977 a congressionally mandated annual report on human rights practices has required the U.S. State Department to detail the offenses committed by allied and hostile governments alike, and a departmental bureau of democracy, human rights, and labor shines the spotlight on uncomfortable places. It is much harder, under such circumstances, for the highest levels of the U.S. government to ignore obvious human rights abuses committed by allied regimes.

Lebanon's "Cedar Revolution," in which 500,000 young street protestors peacefully drove Syrian troops out of the country in March 2005, was possible in part because the intense scrutiny of the international community made intimidation by Syrian-backed security operatives less effective than in the past. Their campaign of assassinations against pro-independence politicians only strengthened the will of the protesters. Lebanese security forces were still present in the streets but stood back and even occasionally facilitated demonstrators' efforts to evade roadblocks and enter the capital to join the protests.

The effects of international attention have likewise increased in the past few years. In 2000 Egyptian democracy activist Saad Eddin Ibrahim was imprisoned after preparing a documentary on voter fraud in Egypt. Western pressure was slow to mount, and Ibrahim was released after three years in jail. But in 2005, when the leader of a new opposition party was arrested on dubious forgery charges after declaring his intention to challenge Hosni Mubarak's planned reinstatement for a sixth unopposed term as president, international media coverage was immediate and the reaction of Western governments swift. The U.S. secretary of state canceled a scheduled trip to Egypt in protest, and the Egyptian foreign minister faced a hostile reception on his previously planned visit to Washington. Opposition leader

Ayman Nour was released within weeks of his arrest, although his trial went forward.[36]

If co-optation is increasingly unaffordable and repression increasingly unsustainable, then rhetoric and ideology designed to evoke public support remain the last refuge of beleaguered Arab leaders. But that tool, too, is now failing Arab autocrats, a casualty of its own inadequacies, the mortality of its greatest champions, and the inevitable competition of information, ideas, and values generated by global trends.

The ouster of Saddam Hussein was a symbolic nail in the coffin of Arab nationalism, but by 2003 the ideology was already increasingly irrelevant to contemporary Arab politics. Arab nationalism suffered first from the repeated military defeat of nationalist leaders at the hands of Israel and then from Egypt's abandonment of Arab unity in the name of national interests in its peace treaty with the Israelis in 1979. When Saddam invaded Kuwait in 1990 and threatened Saudi Arabia, intra-Arab rivalry was on global display, facilitating massive Western intervention and the installation of Western forces in the heart of the Arabian Peninsula in order to expel Iraq's army from Kuwait and contain its future threats to the region. The 1991 Gulf War also created the Kurdish autonomous zone in northern Iraq, ending Saddam's forceful extermination attempts against the Kurds and showcasing for the world the independent aspirations of the region's largest non-Arab minority.

The youth factor is also important in the loosening hold of Arabism as a legitimating ideology for local rulers. As the majority of the region's citizens came to be younger people who did not remember the revolutionary era, the struggles for independence from Western dominance, the 1967 and 1973 wars against Israel, or even the shadow cast over the region by the cold war rivalry of East and West, the anticolonial rhetoric of Arab nationalism became less and less relevant and regimes' reference to external threats seemed less and less persuasive. For younger people, for whom the existence of Israel was a fact of life rather than a recent, artificial imposition, the Arab-Israeli struggle was daily represented by the low-intensity fight for Palestinian independence, not by an image of Arab armies marching en masse to expel the Jewish state from the Arab heartland. Indeed, with the Hashemite Kingdom of Jordan and the Arab Republic of Egypt having signed peace treaties with Israel, young Arabs could be forgiven for thinking that their regimes' protestations of the existential threat represented by Israel rang somewhat hollow. As long-time Arab affairs reporter Yousef Ibrahim put it:

> A stark reality is coursing through Arab consciousness: No one cares about Palestine. . . . Those 300 million Arabs face far more existential concerns. Bad governance, Iraq's potentially infectious sectarian violence, and economic headaches—collapsing stock markets in rich countries and collapsing living standards in poor ones—threaten their survival. Meanwhile, the image of a Palestinian Arab state fades like an old family photo, a yellowish tint deepening around its edges, a nostalgic snapshot rather than a call to arms.[37]

This is not to say that Palestinian rights and Israeli actions are not salient to Arab youths or the broader Arab public—polls clearly show that Arabs continue to rank the Palestinian national struggle high on their lists of political concerns. But the struggle is more distant, complicated by diplomatic efforts at conflict resolution sponsored by Arab governments, and so justice for the Palestinians no longer serves to motivate patriotic loyalty as it did in decades past.

Indeed, justice for Palestine is today just as likely to create resentment and dissent against local Arab governments, because the cry for Palestinian rights has been taken up by opposition Islamists. The resurgence of Islamist opposition movements, beginning in 1979 but especially since the 1991 Gulf War, presented an alternative political ideology that included a comprehensive and devastating critique of existing Arab regimes for their failings in the political, social, economic, and moral realms. I discuss these movements in greater detail in chapter seven. For now it is enough to say that Islamist opposition groups, drawing on an idealized vision of social justice in a golden Islamic past, harp on the inability of today's Arab governments to provide health, education, and other basic social services (along with their inability to produce justice for Palestinians). Islamists further chip away at government legitimacy by providing these services themselves, through voluntary organizations rooted in Islamic principles and bolstered with Islamist ideology. In this way the Islamist critiques of status-quo Arab regimes are both a symptom of the regimes' declining legitimacy and an exacerbator of this trend.

With revolutionary Arab nationalism now discredited as a source for Arab regimes' legitimacy, we are seeing today the emergence of a new era in

Arab politics. In 2006 *Washington Post* correspondent Anthony Shadid commented, "You know, Arab nationalism pretty much doesn't exist anymore. I think even political Islam as a force in which to organize politics around has kind of diminished to a certain extent."[38] With Middle East governments having shifted from anticolonialism to Arab nationalism, and facing a challenge from Islamism, individual Arab regimes' legitimacy will increasingly rest on their ability to perform to public expectations—nothing else is left to turn to as a basis for legitimacy. To survive, Arab states will have to be more self-regarding, less concerned with Arab unity, and ultimately, necessarily, more sensitive to citizen needs. The shift away from pan-Arabism and toward nation-state legitimacy is epitomized in the slogan raised by the Hashemite regime in Jordan after the ascension of King Abdullah (half-British himself, with a Palestinian wife): "Jordan First."[39]

In sum, the Middle East today faces a series of large and growing gaps: between the expectations of a young, more aware generation and the realities they face; between the economic, social, and political gains of most of the rest of the developing world in the past generation and the stagnation of the Arab states; and between the luxurious life of a privileged few who hold political and economic power maintained through corruption and nepotism, on the one hand, and, on the other, the frustration and resentment of the middle class and a growing number of poor, even in the rich oil states of the Persian Gulf.

All this adds up to a recipe for instability. Other indicators tell the same story. The Failed States Index, developed by *Foreign Policy* and the Fund for Peace, evaluates countries' stability according to twelve social, political, and economic indicators. In 2007, 9 Arab states fell into the least-stable half of the 177 states ranked. Iraq, unsurprisingly, ranked second, with a score of 111.4 out of a possible 120 points. But Yemen, Lebanon, Egypt, and Syria all had scores of more than 85 points, placing them in the worst one-quarter of the world in terms of stability. Jordan, Saudi Arabia, Morocco, and Algeria all indicated sufficient problems to rank in the less-stable half of the world (table 3-3). In short, the political status quo in the region—the status quo on which America has long relied to protect its interests—is beginning to crumble. The coming years will see major changes in Arab politics, but these changes may or may not bring about democracy. The upheavals we can foresee can be planned and prepared for and placed in an orderly framework—or they can be chaotic and contentious and possibly dangerous.

Table 3-3. *Failed States Index Scores for Least Stable Countries in the Arab Middle East*

Country	Rank (among 177 states)	Score (out of 120 points)
Iraq	2	111.4
Yemen	24	93.2
Lebanon	28	92.4
Egypt	36	89.2
Syria	40	88.6
Jordan	82	76.6
Saudi Arabia	83	76.5
Morocco	86	76.0
Algeria	89	75.9

Source: "The Failed States Index 2007," Fund for Peace and *Foreign Policy* magazine (www.foreignpolicy.com/story/cms.php?story_id=3865).

Alternatives to a New Social Contract

Most Arab rulers acknowledge that they are facing immense challenges, but they hope to address these challenges through economic reform that will boost growth and through limited openings on the political and social side to relieve the pressure of public demand for change. As I detail in the next chapter, for many of them this is a strategy rooted in wishful thinking rather than socioeconomic reality. Some Arab rulers may succeed in building a China-like model for their countries, in which they produce economic growth and improved welfare for their citizens without yielding any power belonging to the central authority of the king, the state, or the ruling party. But not all of them will. Some of the more populous Arab states, such as Saudi Arabia, Morocco, and Algeria, may fail to achieve the level of economic growth necessary to generate enough new jobs or fail to distribute economic growth in a way that will actually improve people's lives. More likely they will create some new jobs and somewhat more wealth, but corruption will keep those benefits in the hands of a few.

What will happen in Arab states in which governments fail to meet their citizens' needs and expectations? Revolution is one possibility. If a popular revolution were to take place in an Arab country, it would almost certainly be an Islamist revolution, because the Islamist movements are right now the largest grassroots movements in the region. A revolutionary Islamist movement would also likely be a movement that would oppose America's involvement in the region and American interests in fighting terrorism and bringing about Arab-Israeli peace. It seems unlikely that any of the Arab regimes extant today would be toppled by a popular revolution like 1979's Islamic revolution in Iran. No ideological trend or charismatic leader is evident in any Arab country today who could bring people into the streets in the way Nasser and Khomeini did in their respective eras. But revolutions can also come from above, as Nasser himself did: military officers or other elites who feel threatened by change in their societies and stagnation in their governments might effect a coup. Moreover, the Iranian revolution itself was not predicted or expected by analysts in the late 1970s.

One reason social revolutions are unlikely is because Arab governments retain significant capacity to put down such threats with force. Indeed, increased repression is probably the likeliest response by existing governments to their crumbling legitimacy. Although it is costlier for Arab rulers to repress popular dissent today than in the past, it is possible that, faced with large demonstrations or threats of overthrow, some rulers would be willing to use massive repression to keep their thrones. Syria, for example, has already stepped up censorship, surveillance, and arrests of dissident voices or even those offering alternatives to Syria's ongoing confrontation with the international community over its role in Lebanon. We can expect Syria to become even more a police state if international sanctions are put into place to enforce concerns over Lebanon. If its government and its economy, which are already suffering, become even weaker, the state may well turn to increased repression to retain control.

If the governments now ruling in the Arab world feel it necessary to use increasing force at home to repress dissent, that will spur popular support for radical, violent alternatives. If Arab regimes friendly to the United States feel compelled to use greater force domestically in order to keep control, then the United States will also suffer consequences. Governments under that kind of domestic pressure are unlikely to take on additional risk to support the United States on Iraq or the Arab-Israeli peace process. And repression is not a strategy that can be sustained in the long term without consequences such as refugee flows that transcend state borders and potentially threaten regional security. Finally, repression has consequences for regional extremism. In the 1980s and 1990s, Egyptian security services fought a tough campaign against domestic extremists that drove some of those who were not arrested out of the country. Among those who fled abroad was Ayman al-Zawahiri, who became the chief ideologue of al Qaeda.

In a few vulnerable states, political collapse is a possible outcome. The Yemeni government's limited control over rural areas and the border with Saudi Arabia allows organized criminal activity, uncontrolled access to small arms, and terrorist infiltration.[40] The governance failures of the Palestinian Authority in Gaza enabled Hamas's military takeover there, raising the prospect of a terrorist mini-state on the borders of Egypt and Israel. Afghanistan and Somalia provide clear evidence that failed states can present security problems for the larger international community and for the United States. Already the vacuum of governance in Iraq has made the country a magnet for international terrorists who seek a new base of operations against American targets.

A new social contract, rooted in economic and political liberty, is obviously not the only candidate to replace the eroding, unsustainable status quo in today's Middle East. But the nondemocratic alternatives are, from the perspective of American interests, beyond unpalatable. Instability and social revolution threaten to create a more permissive environment for al Qaeda and like-minded groups. Moreover, in this challenging environment, facing severe internal pressure, Arab leaders will find it hard to sustain their cooperation with the United States on issues of common concern without the support of their citizens. In other words, without a shift toward a democratic future, more than Arab stability is threatened—permanent American interests, including core security interests, are threatened as well.

Because of this it is imperative for the United States to play an active role in trying to shape the ways in which Arab governments respond to today's challenges and to help them achieve a new, more stable, and more prosperous future. And in most cases a transition to more democratic politics will be important for ensuring the stability and prosperity of Arab countries and Arab societies. In the next chapter I discuss possible alternative approaches to liberal democratic reform for peacefully resolving the challenges Arab governments face and explain why these alternatives insufficiently address the concerns raised in this chapter about the pressures militating in favor of instability and extremism.

That democracy is the best possible outcome of the region's current ferment is a proposition that garners strong support among Arabs themselves. Arab citizens by and large aspire to democratic change, not to revolutionary overthrow or renewed dictatorship. They show this in polls.[41] And they want it because democracy is no longer just one contender among many but a global norm for enlightened and modern governance and for justice.[42]

Arab regimes recognize that their countries face severe challenges, but so far their responses have been inadequate to the long-term challenge and may in fact increase the risks of negative outcomes such as violence and radicalism. Although the spectrum of their attitudes is broad, most of the twenty-two Arab states themselves recognize their looming challenges and seek to reform—but in ways that improve governmental and economic performance without changing the distribution of political power. Although a few forward-leaning regimes have placed limited power in the hands of their peoples through constitutional and electoral reforms, many others are focused on more cosmetic improvements. The liberalization programs currently embraced by many Arab regimes are intended, from their viewpoint, not to lead to real political competition but to create an impression of progress and, ideally, enhanced prosperity and thereby to mitigate demands from the public for broader political change.[43]

Limited liberalization, however, is insufficient to secure America's interest in marginalizing extremism and promoting long-term stability. It entrenches instead of erodes the privileged position of Islamist radicals as the primary popular opponents to existing Arab regimes, and it will not fully meet the expectations of Arab citizens. As I show in the following chapter, limited liberalization may at best prolong the time in power of unpopular, autocratic leaders whose legitimacy will remain fragile. At worst this approach will enhance Islamists' dominance of the opposition ground. Although not all Islamists are radicals to be feared, an opposition climate dominated by Islamist discourse can only reduce the likelihood that Islamist politicians will feel pressure to conform to the norms of democratic governance. At worst such a situation will expand the market for bin-Ladenist ideas while associating the United States ever more closely with autocratic rulers in an alliance against their citizens' legitimate aspirations for change.

CHAPTER FOUR

Is Democracy
Really Necessary?

T HE DILEMMAS ARAB regimes face today are clear. Over the past three decades, diminished productivity and sluggish growth have combined with population growth and endemic corruption to constrain governments' abilities to penetrate and control society. Even in resource-rich countries, high oil prices do not allow the state to maintain the same level of social services as before, because of unequal distributions of wealth and the high cost of providing education, health care, housing, and jobs for an unusually large young population. The legitimating ideologies Arab rulers have relied on for decades have lost their luster, and repressive tactics have become more costly. Meanwhile, young people, more open than ever to information about the global trends around them, are increasingly aware of the distance between their aspirations and their daily reality and between their prospects and those of young people in other parts of the world. Mounting unemployment, soaring inequality, and persistent nepotism and other forms of corruption give young people little hope that their education and efforts will bring them a brighter future. All these trends, together with the everyday violence in Iraq and the Israeli-Palestinian conflict, have led to the emergence of a young generation in the Arab world whose formative political experience, one U.S. diplomat noted, "has been a decade of bad news, particularly anti-American. . . . Since 1996 it's been one long slide down."[1]

Citizens, especially youth, define their aspirations in social and economic as well as political terms: the ability to have a voice in governance but also the ability to buy an apartment or to marry and have children. Arab autocrats' stability is threatened by the widening gap young people perceive between their aspirations for themselves in the social, economic, and political spheres and their real prospects. The difficulty of integrating a vast young cohort into society is measured not only in creation of new jobs but also in credit and housing and in social freedom (the ability to determine whom one is going to marry and what kind of life one is going to lead) and opportunities for social mobility (the ability to move up from the class in which one was born into something better for one's children). Young people are notoriously impatient, yet conditions are forcing them to wait longer and longer before they can become full adults and begin trying to realize their dreams and plans. In Egypt, for example, marriage costs equate to more than four times the average annual income. But a recent study noted that "while marriage costs have risen with inflation over the years, incomes have been largely stagnant since 1985. With youth unemployment exceeding 30 percent, growing numbers of young Middle Eastern men face serious financial obstacles to getting married, especially in early adulthood. Moroccan men nowadays marry at an average age of 32—seven years later than the previous generation."[2] Unmarried young men, some studies suggest, are especially likely to manifest dissatisfaction with the status quo in politically and socially destructive behavior.[3] The inability of young Arabs to move into adulthood, then, may produce not only an idle population but also an alienated one more vulnerable to mobilization by radical forces.

Although many Arab rulers recognize that the yawning mismatch between their citizens' aspirations and their ability to deliver leaves them in a precarious situation, the very structures they once built to sustain themselves in power now make it costly and risky for them to undertake the reforms in economics, politics, or society that might address mounting public demands and secure the public's continued support for their rule. The changes necessary to create rapid, sustained economic growth and to facilitate improved social mobility seem nearly impossible to bring about without changing the distribution of political power as well. It is increasingly clear that neither the economic reforms necessary for growth and development nor the political reforms necessary for democratization can advance very far in Arab states unless the two are advanced together. Yet the actors whose pressure is required to produce these parallel reforms often work at cross-purposes, leaving constrained and autocratic governments the arbiters of which reforms will occur and on what timetable. The result, in many places, is policymaking paralysis on increasingly urgent questions of political and economic reform. Governments that fail to move far enough, fast enough on reform risk producing destabilizing, dangerous outcomes. The depth of the problem, the apparent inability or unwillingness of governments to make necessary changes, and the dire consequences of failure suggest that external actors have an important role to play.

But what kind of role? The risks in a comprehensive strategy of advancing political, economic, and social reform in the Middle East are real. The possibility that sudden regime change might prove radically destabilizing seems to have been demonstrated in Iraq. The possibility that open elections might bring deeply illiberal, anti-American Islamist movements to power seemed confirmed by the strong showings of several radical Islamist movements in the elections of 2005 and 2006. As I discuss later, both these risks are overblown with regard to the majority of the Arab states. But because of such concerns, American administrations since the end of the cold war have tended to embrace approaches to Arab reform that are designed mainly to minimize risk. Today, too, three main approaches are usually presented as alternatives to a policy of actively promoting comprehensive reform, including democratization:

—Economic development is often asserted to be both a prerequisite and a catalyst for democratic development. Promoting economic development is also presumed to be less confrontational and therefore less costly for the United States in its relations with Arab governments. As a result, some argue for prioritizing economic reforms, in the hope (or on the assumption) that democratization will follow as a natural consequence of economic freedom.

—Some analysts, especially those in the community of "democracy implementers," focus attention on building Arab civil society rather than on pressing for democratic elections. They argue that just as in eastern Europe, indigenous civil society movements in Arab states could effectively and peacefully challenge authoritarian regimes and produce "velvet revolutions." Others argue for the development of civil society by suggesting that it will create a "safer" environment for Arab political competition by building up social groups that can check the power of Islamist movements. To ensure that democratic development goes smoothly, the United States could focus on developing Arab civil society before pressuring Arab governments to open political competition or to share power.

—Some argue that the United States, even if it would prefer comprehensive political and economic reform, must avoid confrontation with valued regional partners and address the perception that it is imposing an agenda on the region. They therefore argue for supporting the efforts at gradual, limited liberalization under way in some Arab states in order to consolidate and stabilize regimes while relieving domestic pressures for farther-reaching changes. Some who advocate this approach assume that gradual liberalization, over time, will prove a slippery slope to democracy.

I examine each of these approaches in turn and explore their prospects for addressing the challenges laid out in chapter three and for protecting core American interests. In the end these less ambitious or less confrontational approaches to promoting Arab reform are largely ineffective and may indeed have unintended negative effects, reinforcing existing problems in the region that threaten America's interests.

Economic Reform First: The Sequencing Trap

Some analysts propose an approach focused on economic rather than political reform, beginning from the premise that economic growth and modernization are important determinants of democratic success.[4] Because pressure for political reform is likely to be resisted by local governments and may produce unintended outcomes, these analysts favor prioritizing economic reform as a good in itself and in the hope that economic progress will ease the path to democratic change.

Reform in the statist, stagnant, corrupt economies of the Arab world is certainly a good in itself. If economic growth can improve sufficiently and if economies can become more open to both global trends and local entrepreneurs, then even poor citizens are likely to see benefits and improvements in their quality of life. And if government regulation of the economy in Arab states can be rationalized and its arbitrariness reduced, that will certainly qualify as a substantive improvement in the quality of Arab governance.

The first problem with an economics-first approach is that given the substantive links in Arab states between economic and political power, economic reform is almost impossible to achieve without also shifting the political status quo in ways that are destabilizing. Governments undertaking economic reforms to liberalize markets and increase competition often face opposition from politically powerful business actors who benefit from the status quo through preferential government contracts, subsidies, or other state protection. These business owners and managers won preferential treatment from the regime in exchange for political support, a classic form of co-optation by autocratic governments. But the largest business actors tend also to be those with the largest stakes in the way government policies are made and enforced. This means that significant liberalizing reforms often risk upsetting large economic actors, which is bad for the economy, and simultaneously alienating powerful political actors, which is bad for the autocrats. One reform-minded Arab minister complained to me that private businesses often demanded "interference positive to them, in terms of intervention, protection, or subsidies or whatever. . . . now they have to give up on that."[5]

This relationship between the structures of economic and political power tend to undermine the private sector's ability to act as an independent force that can challenge or check government power. Especially in Arab countries where liberal political alternatives are small, beleaguered, and denied freedom to operate, business leaders tend to cluster behind the regime, both to preserve their vested interests and to protect against the possibility of a takeover by Islamist movements, which tend to be suspicious of free markets and would likely implement a radical revision of state-business relations in a direction that would harm the private sector. In this way private sector leaders act out of both profit and fear in withholding their support from liberal political forces in society and in preventing reform from acquiring a critical mass of support.

Even Arab governments that might wish to undertake liberal economic reforms face opposition from within their ruling parties and bureaucratic cadres. In Egypt, as in many other Arab countries, ruling party members of parliament rely for local political support on their access to state patronage and their authority to distribute it. Just as in Mayor Richard J. Daley's Chicago, legislators and senior party members dole out civil service jobs, government contracts, the expediting of government decisions, and other preferential treatments in exchange for political support. Legislators and local government officials, then, tend to oppose reforms in state policy that would rationalize or liberalize the provision of state services, because this would also reduce their scope for patronage and threaten their base of support. Similarly, denizens of Arab bureaucratic offices tend firmly to oppose efforts to introduce liberalizing reforms. In addition to the rationale just described, government employees are more directly threatened by losses of position, prestige, and material livelihood when government management of the economy is reduced or when government's role in society is abridged in favor of private actors. An Arab autocrat contemplating significant revisions in economic policy must therefore contend with the possibility that his own civil servants might riot against him—or, at a minimum, work in their jobs to undermine, blunt, or counteract every policy change that comes from the top.

The militaries in Arab states can also play contradictory roles in government-led efforts at reform. On one hand, domestic discontent and the rise of radical ideologies in the region are worrisome to military and security services. As a result, senior officers often support economic changes that they believe can increase social stability.[6] On the other hand, the military and security services in most Arab states consume a tremendous share of government resources, and the military sector may also manage factories and other government-owned businesses that would be targets of any serious structural reforms. Military elites therefore have their own vested interests in the economic status quo, and their capacity to shape politics—demonstrated in the number of military-led coups the region has witnessed—makes leaders wary of discomfiting them through reforms that touch closely on their interests.

The problem of vested interests binding the hands of Arab rulers is exacerbated by the higher expectations they now face both at home and abroad. Global expectations have shifted as consensus has grown about the policy environment necessary for economic growth, raising the bar above which domestic economic reforms will receive a positive response from global capital markets and international donor agencies. Although high oil prices have meant that more local capital is available for investment, it does not necessarily follow that pressure for structural reforms is reduced: wealthy gulf Arabs still seek security and a good return on their money and can easily direct their funds to other, more favorable business environments outside the region. Moreover, as Arab citizens have enjoyed greater access to new information about the world around them, their expectations and aspirations for reform have also escalated, upping the ante for nervous governments attempting to revise the social contract and still preserve themselves in power.

The problem of vested interests means that economic reform often threatens the political foundations of autocratic Arab regimes just as much as outright political reform would do. Although it is possible to find Arab rulers who desire to improve their countries' economic prospects, it is rare to find Arab rulers who are willing to do so at the expense of their own rule. As Thomas Carothers remarked, "despite some commitment to socioeconomic progress, such leaders may also be fixated on enriching themselves, protecting certain privileged groups or sectors in the society, and undercutting potential political rivals."[7] For this reason economic reforms have in recent years been carried out only slowly and halfheartedly in places where they have been attempted at all, and they have just as often been reversed.

Economic reform by itself, then, is likely to be as problematic for Arab autocrats as political reform. Although their incentives may appear to be stronger in the economic domain, their interests are in the end just as resolutely opposed. But there is an additional problem with embracing economic change as the main thrust of an American policy to help stabilize the Arab states of the Middle East: economic reform alone is likely to prove insufficient to achieve the American goal of ameliorating an environment in which extremism and terrorism can find succor. Some academics have long argued that poverty and material deprivation are the drivers of political violence, yet this clearly was not the case with the al Qaeda terrorists who carried out the attacks of September 11, 2001, or their colleagues in London and Madrid. Rather, as Olivier Roy has shown in his research into the roots of international jihadism, bin-Ladenist terrorists emanate from the educated middle classes, and their indoctrination into the ideology of jihadism is a consequence of their social, political, and spiritual dislocation more than of any material lack.[8] Certainly the lack of employment for educated young men increases the available pool of idle, dissatisfied, and resentful youths on which opposition or protest movements can draw. But it alone does not turn men into terrorists.

If economic reform alone is insufficient to combat the conditions that breed extremism in Arab society, cannot economic liberalization still be employed as the thin edge of a wedge for broader political change? Those who argue in this direction note that the changes in laws, institutions, and procedures that help to nurture economic growth in an era of globalized markets and trade ought also to aid the growth of democracy. As Richard Haass put it, "the elements required in a modern economy—the rule of law, transparency, room for individual initiative—are exactly the same things that a modern democracy requires."[9] Similarly, Fareed Zakaria has argued that "the process of economic development usually produces the two elements that are crucial to the success of liberal democracy. First, it allows key segments of society—most important, private businesses and the broader bourgeoisie—to gain power independent of the state. Second, in bargaining with these elements the state tends to become less rapacious and capricious and more rule-oriented and responsive to society's needs, or at least to the needs of the elite of that society. This process results in liberalization, often unintentionally."[10] Advocates of economic reform as a means to democratic reform often cite the cases of Taiwan and South Korea, where the growth of the private sector and a growing middle class helped produce new demands for political rights and, eventually, peaceful democratic transitions.

There are reasons to doubt, however, that autocrats do quite as good a job of building these foundations for democracy as Zakaria and Haass suppose. The vested interests discussed earlier are a key reason. As Carothers pointed out, "many autocrats have some interest in developing their country, but they subordinate it to other interests that not only compromise their socioeconomic policies but undermine any serious pursuit of the rule of law." Arab regimes have interests in maintaining political support through state-directed largesse, and "these other interests usually require deforming the rule of law in significant, even systematic ways."[11] The empirical record—both of countries that have liberalized and those that have not—does not support the sequencing thesis, either. In states that have built strong rules of law, commercial sector reforms have not led the way. And, Carothers noted, "careful analyses of whether the spreading of reforms across domains is actually happening in countries such as China have been reaching skeptical conclusions."[12]

The Arab states may in fact be particularly ill suited to a strategy of economics-first sequencing. The notion that newly independent middle classes will rise to demand their political rights from governments may not hold for the oil-rich states of the Middle East or indeed for other Arab states that enjoy government income from external rents. In these countries the government plays a massive role in the national economy because it can easily achieve sizable revenues from sales of state-managed energy resources. This government-controlled revenue stream allows the authorities to sustain significant social welfare subsidies without taxation. The effect of these oil rents (and in other cases, strategic rents in the form of Western military and economic aid) tends to keep all economic classes, but especially the white-collar middle class, dependent on the state and thus reduces the likelihood of a South Korean–style middle-class mobilization for political freedom.

Tunisia offers a case study of how Western-encouraged economic reforms that produced impressive economic growth and jolts of foreign investment have still not loosened the grip of one of the region's most effective police states, because of the dependence of private sector actors on the beneficence of overwhelming government authority. Eva Bellin has reported that in Tunisia "the state explicitly nourishes the development of private sector capital and labor. . . . State sponsorship fosters the development of capital and labor but also undermines [people's] enthusiasm for democracy. Classes that have benefited from state sponsorship often exhibit a 'pulling up the ladder' syndrome. They are eager to push the state to be responsive to their own interests, but once this has been achieved, they are not eager to generalize such responsiveness to society as a whole through the creation of democratic institutions."[13] Middle Eastern regimes such as Tunisia see China rather than South Korea as their East Asian model, because the Chinese state has facilitated economic liberalization and sustained tremendous growth without meaningfully opening up its politics.[14]

Indeed, the destabilizing effects of economic reforms designed to improve growth, create jobs, and attract investment can induce countries to *de*-liberalize their politics rather than the opposite. The stop-and-go history of economic reforms in Egypt in recent years provides clear evidence for this thesis. In 1991, following an economic crisis caused in part by a drop in oil prices, the government of Egypt committed to a macroeconomic stabilization package in an agreement with the International Monetary Fund that included adjusting the valuation of currency, reducing public spending, and privatizing state-owned businesses. But the reforms promised painful dislocations for many Egyptian workers. Saad Eddin Ibrahim observed that "with family members of all the civil servants and public-sector employees taken into account, the required measures promised to have an immediate effect on as many as 25 million Egyptians. With tension and violence already on the rise in the form of confrontations with Islamic militants, the government found itself unable or unwilling to risk alienating so many citizens. These fears were not without justification. Labor unrest, as measured by the numbers of strikes, demonstrations, and acts of sabotage, increased eighteen-fold from 1990 to 1993."[15] As the political costs of economic change began to rise in the mid-1990s, economic reforms slowed to a crawl.

After a ten-year pause, the government of Egypt was desperate for foreign investment and faced strong pressure from the American Congress, which had conditioned a portion of Egypt's economic assistance on new reform measures. President Mubarak appointed a new cabinet with a reform mandate, and it haltingly began to implement a new round of structural reforms in 2004. The government floated the Egyptian pound, radically revised customs and income tax laws, and prepared a new set of government businesses for privatization. But even as these reforms got under way, those closest to the issue expressed their skepticism that the regime's commitment to economic restructuring could be sustained long enough to produce noticeable gains for the average Egyptian. Cabinet members pleaded with businessmen enjoying new relief from taxes and import duties to invest their increased profits in employment-generating business rather than profit-taking.[16] Business actors may in principle favor these liberalizing reforms, but their interest in social stability is also threatened by the social forces that reform can unleash. At times business actors may even condone regime retrenchment or repression in order to avoid the destabilizing effects of political or economic change. The private sector may thus serve to sustain the roller-coaster cycle of political liberalization evident in many Arab countries.

As Eberhard Kienle noted with regard to the Egyptian experience, the dislocation engendered by the reforms of the 1990s led to mass protests and greater activism by unions and other affected social groups. This led the regime to establish new restrictions on unions, the press, and political parties to contain expressions of dissent and ensure an overwhelming victory for the ruling party in the 1995 parliamentary elections. Kienle concluded that "political deliberalization was the immediate corollary of reforms that were meant to enhance property rights, increase private sector growth, and otherwise liberalize the economy."[17]

The preceding analysis suggests that efforts at economic reform in the Arab states are deeply constrained by the problem of vested interests; that economic reform alone—even if undertaken with fervor—will not suffice to address American concerns about regional radicalization; and that economic reform will not necessarily improve the prospects for rule of law or other democratic reforms down the road. Indeed, the lesson of previous Arab experiences with economic liberalization is that unless political and economic reforms are undertaken in tandem, there is no compelling reason to expect that the latter will provoke the former.[18] Their past experience leads some Egyptian reformers to suggest that in the absence of accompanying political liberalization to enable debate of economic policy and to provide alternative sources of legitimacy for the regime, fundamental economic reform is impossible.[19]

The Civil Society Myth

Civil society is a second focus for those seeking to alleviate the risks of U.S. democracy promotion in the Arab world. Given the resistance Arab regimes have demonstrated to external pressures for democratic reform, and given the ruptured alliances or outright instability that intensified pressures for reform might produce, some analysts argue that the United States should take a more indirect approach to promoting change. Pointing to the lack of a history of democratic politics in the Arab world, the relative immaturity of political institutions such as parliaments and political parties, and the danger of Islamist populism, these observers advocate a focus on building up indigenous social organizations and creating a democratic culture before pressing for procedural democracy. Moreover, faced with recalcitrant governments that resist top-down reform, the argument goes, the United States risks losing strategic cooperation and encourages perceptions of America as imposing its own system on local societies. Some argue that the United States should instead set aside pressure for structural changes in politics and work to empower indigenous civil society groups, which can raise their own internal demands for change. With proper encouragement and training, some suggest, Arab civil society can produce velvet revolutions in Damascus and Cairo just as eastern European dissidents did in Prague and Budapest.

It is true that civil society is a crucial element in mature democracies and that civil society organizations in other places and times have played central roles in inducing democratic transitions in their countries. Cultivating civil society is a positive step in principle, but conditions in Arab countries make it difficult in practice to view the promotion of civil society as the central facet of a pro-reform strategy in the Middle East.

The argument in favor of civil society assistance is seductive, particularly in light of the illiberal outcomes of elections in Iraq, the Palestinian territories, and Lebanon in 2005 and 2006—in all of which armed Islamist sectarian movements garnered significant parliamentary representation. These results led many observers to argue that the problem with President Bush's policy of democracy promotion was its emphasis on elections first, rather than on building social supports for democracy and inculcating liberal values through civic education.[20] Such critics assumed that building a "democratic culture" would prevent illiberal political forces such as Hizballah from succeeding at the ballot box. As I show in chapter six, however, the militants' electoral success had less to do with the absence of democratic culture and civil society than with the absence of effective governance. Observers who argue for the promotion of civil society before or instead of elections draw the wrong lesson from these cases.

Moreover, such questions of sequencing political reforms—putting constitutional reform and civic growth ahead of elections, for example—are seldom relevant to U.S. policy in the Middle East. They are useful when applied to situations of state collapse and reconstruction, as in Bosnia, or to situations of occupation, as in Iraq.[21] But in functioning, sovereign states, whether authoritarian or democratic, external actors such as the United States rarely have much influence over when an election is held. This is especially true when, as has been the case across the Middle East, autocratic executives regularly set up highly controlled elections as a means of containing public demands for political participation and of legitimating their continued rule.

Not only are external judgments about ideal sequencing often irrelevant to actual political circumstances, but experience shows that different types of political reforms can interact in positive and sometimes unexpected ways, making the notion that an ideal "sequence" exists difficult to sustain. The scheduling of an election in Egypt in 2005, for example, opened up new avenues for the development of civil society in areas such as voter education and election monitoring, along with providing a good pretext for American assistance to civic groups and American pressure on the Egyptian regime to increase media freedom. Although the Egyptian government scaled back many of these changes immediately after the elections concluded, the gains for freedom were real and palpable to local activists. With these sorts of possibilities on offer, it would be strange indeed for the United States to decide a priori to downplay election prospects in favor of an "under-the-radar" approach.

An additional question is what American civil society assistance actually does for local civic activists. For the most part, before giving operational grants to local groups, American and other Western funders work to build civic groups' "capacity"—that is, their internal organization and the managerial and budgetary capability to handle American money with the diligence expected by American appropriators in Congress. One North African activist told me that American civil society assistance projects propose "to help us be more efficient, to organize. But there is something before this— to have the *right* to organize."[22]

Most Arab states severely restrict freedom of association, making it difficult for civic activists to meet and organize, much less demonstrate for change. Nongovernmental organizations (NGOs) are often required by local laws to acquire explicit government approval for their establishment, bylaws, boards of directors, and budgets—approval that can be withdrawn at any time. Where NGOs are allowed to exist, they are often barred from political activity or from accepting foreign funds.[23] Civic groups with potentially political roles, such as labor unions, professional syndicates, and human rights organizations, are heavily monitored by government, penetrated by domestic intelligence services, and subjected to swift repression through legal or police means when they undertake independent political action.

As a result of these constraints, the great majority of civic groups in the Arab world tend to be small and restricted to innocuous activities such as providing social services to the poor. Egypt boasts more than 10,000 civil society organizations, but most of them are politically irrelevant. Arab NGOs that do work specifically on democracy, human rights, and other political issues are constantly monitored, harassed, and under threat. Although pro-democracy NGOs exist in almost every country in the region, they may be dependent on foreign support (financial, political, or both) and are often marginal in their ability to affect public perceptions and popular demands on government. They have little prospect of cultivating a popular pro-democracy movement or producing a "people-power" revolution. Without external pressure on regimes to allow political organization to proceed, civil society has little hope of challenging the balance of power in any single Arab state. And there is no framework like the Helsinki Agreement to provide cover for such activists to challenge these internal constraints.[24]

In the end, no matter how many small-bore grants the U.S. government gives to improve parliamentary effectiveness, judicial independence, or the rule of law, the legislatures and judiciaries in most Arab countries will remain subordinated to their executives—until those executives are persuaded or compelled to give up emergency laws and restrain security forces. No matter how much training the National Endowment for Democracy sponsors for new citizens' movements or liberal politicians, they will be unable to compete in the political marketplace until their governments allow freedom of expression and association. The gap between the small-scale technical assistance that Western donors provide and the political pressure it will take to induce real devolution of power by autocratic regimes is too large. In other words, civil society assistance can have real effects only when accompanied by changes within the regimes themselves that will give pro-democracy civic groups the freedom to organize and act. This is nearly impossible to imagine without concerted external pressure, including pressure from the United States, on behalf of fundamental political freedoms.

Gradual Liberalization: Building a Kinder, Gentler Autocracy

The understandable desire of Arab autocrats to retain the power and privileges of their positions is obviously the greatest barrier to democratic development in the region. But if Arab rulers are aware of the demographic, economic, and legitimacy challenges they are facing, could they not be persuaded to undertake some self-serving reforms to stabilize their own rule? Some argue that the United States, instead of risking alienation from Arab allies by pressing them on democracy and human rights, should instead support their efforts at self-preservation through limited liberalizing reform. With luck such top-down, gradual liberalization might in time evolve into democratization. At least, these voices argue, liberalization will relieve the rising public demands for change and stabilize the status quo.

For a long time before September 11, 2001, the United States government took the view that the best alternative to an assertive pro-democracy push was supporting a gradual liberalization of politics, led from the top by enlightened rulers. This option is still embraced by those who emphasize the United States' inability to impose democracy on unwilling autocrats and by those who see the fact of governance, rather than its nature, as the crucial determinant of world order and chief securer of American national interests. Robert Kaplan, for example, sees the post–cold war years as having opened a Pandora's box of long-simmering problems of political order: ethnic identities, resource wars, and fragile social institutions in developing countries that threaten global peace and security. He sees the main problem in the Middle East as one of sustaining order rather than building democracy: "What we have to work toward—for which peoples with historical experiences different from ours will be grateful—is not democracy but normality. . . . The more cautious we are in a world already in the throes of tumultuous upheaval, the more we'll achieve."[25]

This preference for strengthening the existing order and following the lead of the region's current rulers is also evident in the view, promulgated by Brent Scowcroft and quoted in the last chapter, that alliance with Arab monarchs and dictators has served American interests well for decades. If economic or social problems are undermining these rulers' strength, then the response of the United States should not be to press for a transition to democracy but rather to support the powers-that-be by providing economic, technical, and trade incentives to help them address these problems and rebuild their rule on a more stable foundation. Finally, there are those who argue that Arab societies are not "prepared" for democracy in some cultural or historical sense—that Arab citizens accustomed to paternalistic autocracy would be uncomfortable with a sudden shift to public participation in governance. Gradual liberalization is a way to inculcate the political and social values of modernity without the upsetting consequences for social order that swift democratization might produce.[26]

All these advocates treat gradual liberalization as a more pragmatic and less confrontational means to achieving democratic change than the Bush administration's aggressively rhetorical policy. They argue that America's primary relationships in the Middle East have always been with the regimes, not with liberal or other political alternatives, and that the United States, because of its ties to autocrats and the unpopularity of its regional policies, lacks the capacity to connect with or help build a democratic opposition that could challenge regimes to loosen their controls over politics. American assistance to Arab liberals, in this view, is the best way to torpedo their domestic credibility and ensure their failure in attracting public support. These voices argue that any effective reform policy will have to be carried out in cooperation with the regimes. Over time, they suggest, the infiltration of liberal values and the modernization of Arab society through educational and economic progress will make democracy both more likely and less threatening.[27]

In fact, many Arab rulers have embarked on programs of liberalization, some limited to the economic sphere, some comprising reforms in social legislation (such as the Moroccan personal status law, the Mudawwana, advanced by King Mohammed VI), and some offering limited expansion of political participation (such as Egypt's newly competitive presidential elections and the United Arab Emirates' new semi-elected consultative council). It is necessary to be frank and fair in assessing the intentions and limitations of these hesitant experiments in liberalization.[28] If the limited goals and likely even more limited effects of such top-down programs can indeed deliver stability and longevity for Arab regimes and perhaps even lay the groundwork for later democratic transitions, then surely gradual, regime-led liberalization is the best approach for the United States to endorse.

But limited liberalization is unlikely to lead to sufficient economic, political, and social progress to stabilize Arab regimes in the face of the pressures they currently confront. As I discussed earlier, Arab autocrats face political difficulties in implementing economic liberalization, difficulties that have already curtailed or slowed promising liberalization schemes. But the conflicts autocrats face between their interest in modernizing governance and their interest in remaining as governor exist across policy domains: in combating corruption, advancing the impartial rule of law, and cultivating effective budgetary accountability. In these and other domains, liberalizing reforms can threaten the foundations of political support for autocratic rule or the core mechanisms autocrats use to maintain power. Liberalizing reforms, then, are unlikely to extend far enough, for long enough, to address either mounting public demands for improved governance or the demands of investors and global markets for a better business climate.

For the same reason it is unlikely that, as some advocates of gradualism hope, liberalization over time will take on such momentum that autocratic Arab regimes will no longer be able to avoid real devolution of power—that is, that limited liberalization is a slippery slope toward democratization.

Even if well-founded, this hope also carries risk: if the regimes lose control, the outcome might be chaotic, and there is no guarantee that the region's long-suppressed liberals will win out. More realistically, if past history is any guide, efforts at controlled liberalization are as likely as not to be quickly shut down or reversed when their social effects spiral out of control or when public appetites for change are whetted rather than dulled by the regime's cautious steps. To take one example, Jordan in the early 1990s embarked on a program of political and economic reform, but when the government reduced wheat subsidies and lifted price controls, riots quickly escalated across the south. In an immediate crackdown the king dismissed parliament and instituted new restrictions on press freedom. In protest, opposition groups boycotted the 1997 parliamentary elections, and Jordanian political liberalization has largely been stalled ever since.[29]

Similarly, the young emir of Bahrain, at his ascension to the throne in 1999, promised to restore parliamentary democracy under a new constitution and bring about greater equality between the ruling Sunnis and the majority Shiites. These reforms were encapsulated in the national charter approved by Bahrain's electorate in 2001. Important Shiite groups boycotted the local and parliamentary elections held in 2002, after the new constitution was revealed, because it created an appointed upper house of parliament to blunt the power of the elected lower house. In 2006, after several years of U.S.-government-funded activism and development among Bahraini human rights and democracy activists, Shiite groups resolved not to boycott the elections but to participate and use parliament as a platform to further the cause of sectarian equality and open democracy.[30] The Bahraini government then created a new government-run human rights council stacked with regime loyalists and passed new legislation requiring all Bahraini NGOs to work under its umbrella. Foreign funding outside this mechanism was prohibited, and one American NGO that disputed the new constraints was compelled to suspend activity when its representative was denied permission to return to the country.[31] Arab rulers, then, do not appear vulnerable to gradualism as a "stealth democratization strategy."

The case of Morocco suggests further that limited liberalization, even when it appears to go smoothly, does not necessarily improve the long-term stability of regimes worried about frustrated publics and the threat of extremism. In 1999 the young King Mohammed VI succeeded his aged father and launched a relatively ambitious program of political and social reforms. He loosened press controls, opened registration for political parties, and even launched an Equity and Reconciliation Commission to examine human rights abuses during the regime of his father, Hassan II.

Over the last several years, major social reforms have helped cultivate a more liberal culture in Morocco. Notable among them are an overhaul of the family code that enhances women's rights in marriage, divorce, and citizenship and an agreement among political parties to reserve slots on a special national parliamentary ballot for women. Morocco also has a history of peaceful pluralism so firm that the population still includes several thousand Jews, who enjoy genuine freedom of worship and close ties to Israel. Moroccan society also generally takes a relatively mellow approach to Islam, wherein veiled women and those wearing tank tops dine comfortably together in the many sidewalk cafes of the capital. Morocco boasts what is arguably the most moderate—at least on its face—Islamist party in the Arab world, one that consciously models itself on Europe's Christian Democrats and the pro–European Union Party of Justice and Development (PJD) in Turkey. There are hard questions to be asked about the sincerity of the PJD's commitment to pluralism, but if Islamism and democracy can ever be proved compatible, it might well be in Morocco.

Yet Morocco's political liberalization has significant limits. Complicated electoral laws ensure that parliamentary seats are fairly evenly distributed, regardless of who wins the largest share of the national vote, and parliamentary powers are so overshadowed by the king's legislative authority that few members of parliament (with the notable exception of the Islamist opposition) even bother to show up when the body is in session. Instead, some use their parliamentary status and the legal immunity it grants them to advance their own narrow interests and sometimes to cover criminal activity. Ultimately, despite its progress, Moroccan democracy remains a shadow game: democratic institutions have little substantive authority, and citizens' preferences, as expressed at the ballot box, rarely have much effect on government policy.

The outcome of the 2007 parliamentary elections in Morocco suggests that the country's citizens clearly understand this game and are tired of playing it. Despite a massive voter registration and mobilization campaign, barely 37 percent of the registered population turned up to vote—and of those, about one fifth deliberately spoiled their ballots, some scrawling antigovernment messages across the ballot papers.[32] This act of political protest suggests that limited liberalization, even in the best of circumstances, has a limited life span with frustrated citizens.

The young king is left with a difficult choice. There are forces in Morocco ready and eager to take advantage of the voters' increasing disaffection. In addition to the PJD, another Islamist group, the banned Justice and Charity Association, calls the current system useless and demands an end to the monarchy. Even worse, homegrown Islamist terrorism has increased, notwithstanding the efforts of Morocco's efficient domestic security services, flush with U.S. funding and training. The 2004 Madrid train bombings, almost certainly carried out by Moroccans, are perhaps the most notorious example, but in 2007 alone three Moroccan suicide bombers detonated themselves in the country's tourist-filled cities.

To engage voters, King Mohammed would have to strengthen parliament and the mainstream political parties, giving them a real capacity to act on voters' concerns and reducing his own power in the process. If he chooses not to fortify parliament, he faces the risk that voters may abandon their faith in the democratic process and turn to more dangerous and destabilizing alternatives. The king's difficult choices suggest that erecting the forms of democracy without much substance, a balance now well developed in Morocco, may not ultimately win the loyalty of Arab citizens. And if democratic forms lose legitimacy, then tightly managed liberalization, far from ensuring stability in a dangerous environment, may end up pushing Arab societies away from peaceful politics altogether and further into the arms of extremists.

If the United States is concerned to counter the social roots of radicalism and to advance liberal alternatives to the political rhetoric of violent Islamists, then the biggest risk in a gradualist strategy is in fact the absence of substantive political change. By design the regimes' top-down liberalization does not relax state control sufficiently to enable the formation of any organized political alternative to the state itself or to Islamist opposition movements, who are often vague in their platforms and their commitments to basic democratic norms such as nonviolence and equality before the law. These Islamist movements have long enjoyed the ability to use the mosque as a place to organize, whereas other arenas of social organization have long been tightly restricted by the autocratic regime. In this way the regimes have maintained control—and also maintained the Islamist opposition as the only large, well-organized alternative to their rule. The Islamists' dominance of the opposition ground serves as the excuse many regimes give Washington to explain why truly free politics is too dangerous and why political liberalization can go only so far and no farther.

The longer the U.S. government rewards and encourages regimes that "liberalize" without allowing new political forces to develop, the more existing Islamist movements benefit from the limited political openings that do exist. The more entrenched these Islamists become as the dominant political alternative to the status quo, the more the language of Islamism becomes the language of protest politics and the more other voices become marginalized. Unchallenged by other opposition voices, Islamists need not clarify their vague statements on central questions such as the legitimacy of violent "resistance," the status of women and minorities, and the role of religious authority in governance. The net effect of controlled liberalization, then, may be not to "drain the swamp" of extremist rhetoric and the justifications for violence that emanate from it but to expand the swamp instead. Gradual liberalization is thus the likeliest path to ensuring that open politics in the Arab world, when it does arrive, will be of a particularly illiberal, anti-Western, and irresponsible variety.

At best, then, limited liberalization may prolong the duration in power of unpopular, autocratic leaders whose legitimacy will remain fragile. At worst this approach will enhance Islamists' dominance of the opposition ground and create a broader and more susceptible market for radical, bin-Ladenist ideas while associating the United States ever more closely with autocratic rulers in an alliance against their citizens' legitimate aspirations for change. That said, proponents of gradual liberalization are right in one thing: that America's main leverage is with regimes, not with Arab citizens. Given the current levels of mistrust and resentment of American foreign policy among average Arabs, that will not likely change in the near term. Thus any American reform strategy must include an effective and sustainable approach to Arab autocrats who have long been America's friends and allies.

CHAPTER FIVE

The Bush Record

S o FAR I have sought to demonstrate the need for the United States to undertake a major, long-term, comprehensive effort to advance economic, political, and social reform in Arab countries, in order to protect core American interests and promote the region's long-term stability and prosperity. But that a thing should be done and that it can be done are two distinct claims. What if, despite all the best reasons and intentions, the United States cannot play an effective and positive role in shaping the direction and outcome of the changes that are sweeping the Arab world and will continue in years to come?

The record built by the George W. Bush administration gives little reason for optimism in this regard. The disastrous adventure in Iraq, unfortunately, made democracy promotion in the Middle East synonymous with forceful regime change, and the failure of the Iraqi reconstruction effort produced a concomitant backlash against democratization regionwide. Elections held by three of the region's weakest governments—Iraq, Lebanon, and the Palestinian Authority—produced strong gains for militant Islamist movements that place narrow interests and ideology above national unity and well above the rule of law. Even in the stronger states of the region, such as Egypt, elections produced gains for nonviolent Islamist movements. In the face of these outcomes, and alongside major strategic crises with Iran, in Iraq, and in the Israeli-Palestinian conflict, the Bush administration abandoned any ambitious efforts to promote democracy in its waning days and shifted to a rhetoric that prioritized diplomatic cooperation with "moderate allies" such as Mubarak and the King Abdullahs of Jordan and Saudi Arabia against the region's myriad security challenges.

The meager results and lost momentum of America's democracy push in the Middle East over the Bush years derived from two sources. First, American interventions on behalf of democratic progress in the Arab world were not, for the most part, well designed or well targeted—indeed, they seemed to proceed in a rather ad hoc manner. This lack of coherent strategy was perhaps most evident in the statement by then deputy assistant secretary of state Scott Carpenter that "we don't know yet how best to promote democracy in the Arab Middle East. I mean we just don't know. It's the early days. . . . I think there are times when you throw spaghetti against the wall and see if it sticks."[1] Second, Bush's efforts to promote democracy, even when direct and powerful, were subverted in their effect by a generalized lack of policy support and high-level engagement from across the U.S. government. Both the incoherence and the inconsistency of the Bush administration's efforts were products of an underlying ambivalence about the project—ambivalence due to the failure of the Bush administration, like those before it, to resolve the dilemmas relating to conflicts of interest and Islamism that are inherent in U.S. democracy promotion in the Middle East.

The United States cannot afford to take a neutral stance in the face of the region's mounting governance and legitimacy challenges and the stalemated efforts by Arab regimes to address them. September 11, 2001, clearly changed the calculus for President Bush and his advisers regarding the urgency of Arab reform, leading to his landmark declaration of a "forward strategy of freedom" in the Middle East. But over the course of his administration, too, America's bold intentions with respect to Arab democracy were blunted repeatedly by the real and perceived risks of fundamental change in the region. The conflict-of-interests problem and the Algeria problem described in chapter two infected Bush administration policy just as thoroughly as the policies of its predecessors, and in the end his administration's actions came nowhere near matching his soaring rhetoric, either in implementation or in effects.

Over the course of Bush's years in office, the discontinuities in American policy toward Middle Eastern democracy were striking, raising questions about the depth and sustainability of the U.S. government's commitment to democracy promotion in the Arab world. President Bush personally called

Hosni Mubarak in the spring of 2005 to voice his expectations for a freer press and independent monitoring of Egypt's planned elections, and the U.S. embassy in Cairo gave independent funding to Egyptian nongovernmental organizations (NGOs) for the first time that year. Just six months later the U.S. State Department's muted reaction to Mubarak's intimidation of judges, jailing of protestors, postponement of local elections, and renewal of emergency laws left observers puzzled. This inconsistency further damaged American credibility, but it also raised two pointed questions: Can a bold American pro-democracy drive in the Middle East be sustained in the face of setbacks like Mubarak's backsliding or increased costs like the election victory of Palestinian Hamas? And can the Freedom Agenda— described by its authors as a generational commitment—survive the end of Bush's term in office?

A detailed assessment of the work done by the Bush administration to advance the Freedom Agenda in the Middle East is required to answer these questions fairly. Only in light of such an analysis can one distinguish just how much did and did not change in the United States' approach to the autocratic politics of Arab leaders and how much the country must yet invest in order to promote the democratic transformation of the Middle East. In this chapter I discuss how the Bush administration's firm intentions failed: how the conflict-of-interests problem and the Islamist problem pushed American officials to seek means to advance Arab democratic reform that they thought could avoid these problems, and how those alternative approaches repeatedly failed to yield the desired results. Indeed, in its quest to avoid the conflict-of-interests problem, the Bush administration made choices and took steps that probably exacerbated the Algeria problem and set back the cause of democracy regionwide. Following this look at the way Bush's Freedom Agenda, like previous efforts, fell prey to these two dilemmas, I explore ways in which they can be addressed to build a pro-reform policy that is realistic, sustainable, and ultimately effective.

One might wonder whether, if even an administration as committed as Bush's cannot overcome the Algeria and conflict-of-interests problems, any administration can. Perhaps, despite America's clear interest in Arab democracy, its government is simply too ill equipped and ill positioned to play a positive role in this regional drama. In chapters six and seven I take on this challenge, framing an alternative American approach that, instead of avoiding these two crucial questions, confronts and resolves them, thus enabling sustained and coherent American efforts to help the Arab world address its mounting challenges and build a more stable and prosperous future.

In its early years the Bush administration made significant progress in its efforts to shift U.S. policy toward supporting democratic reform in Arab politics. In 2004 and 2005 the administration's new rhetoric and commitment to new programs such as the Middle East Partnership Initiative and the Broader Middle East and North Africa Initiative of the Group of Eight leading world economies (G8), combined with growing internal pressures for reform, coaxed a noticeable change in attitude—if not in intentions—out of Arab governments. In February 2004, when a U.S. proposal for a G8-sponsored Middle East reform program was leaked to a newspaper, major Arab leaders such as Egypt's President Mubarak felt comfortable rejecting the concept out of hand as imperialist and irrelevant.[2] By 2006, however, virtually every Arab government has formally committed to participating in some aspect of the same G8 initiative. The Bush administration also succeeded, for a time, in engaging Western allies in a continuing discussion of Middle East democracy and how to achieve it.

But although these early actions may have persuaded Arab governments that the Bush commitment to regional democratization was sincere, they failed to convince Arab rulers and other observers that the effort was serious. This was mainly because the Bush administration was never able to delineate how it would handle perceived trade-offs between the long-term project of democracy promotion and shorter-term imperatives such as counterterrorism cooperation, assistance in stabilizing Iraq, and support for the Middle East peace process. Instead of confronting the conflict-of-interests problem head-on, Bush and his advisers sought to avoid it by directing their fiercest pro-democracy diplomacy toward countries whose governments were too weak to resist, by downplaying diplomacy with Arab allies on basic political rights, and by directing most U.S. democracy assistance to a variety of blunt-edged programs that had little potential to change Arab politics over time. Bush's Freedom Agenda was never able to develop an approach to Middle East democracy promotion that merged diplomacy and assistance in a mutually reinforcing strategy or that rooted democracy promotion deeply in the institutions and daily conduct of U.S. foreign policy. Because of the failure to resolve the conflict-of-interests problem at home and abroad, Bush officials made a series of misjudgments and when met with failure quickly began to reverse course. The end result was a loss of credibility, not only for the Freedom Agenda but for U.S. democracy promotion generally.

Pushing Weak Governments Hardest: A Recipe for Failure

The first and most fundamental problem with the Bush administration's approach was its choice of focus for its democracy promotion efforts. The early years of the twenty-first century saw promising political developments in countries around the Middle East. Domestic demands for political change were mounting, and internal pro-democracy movements were becoming increasingly organized, vocal, and specific in their demands on their governments. In part these developments were the result of shifts in the local and regional environment, as discussed in chapter three. In part, also, the ability of these indigenous movements to mount public campaigns for liberal political reform was bolstered by training and support from Western implementers of democracy assistance, who had been working quietly in the region for some years.

The Bush administration took note of progress and potential in countries such as Morocco, where debates over parliamentary power and Islamist participation were brewing, and Egypt, where a new liberal party won legal recognition in the courts and immediately announced that it would field a candidate for the presidency. The U.S. government voiced rhetorical support for such efforts and even gave some of them technical or financial assistance. But seldom did it do the single most important thing it could have done to advance the prospects of these indigenous democrats: press the governments in these countries to allow local movements to operate more freely. That is, it did not press governments to create an environment of increased political freedom in which these groups could do their work with greater ease and to greater effect. Low-level training and assistance programs could not make up for the deficit of political freedoms in these societies, and progress in these places has stalled or even reversed.

The Bush administration chose instead to focus its political capital and its highest-profile pro-democracy diplomacy on places where governance was severely challenged: Iraq (perforce), Lebanon, and the Palestinian territories. More specifically, it focused on implementing democratic processes, mainly elections, in weak states rather than prioritizing political freedoms in strong states where democratic progress was possible. Weak states (or nonstates, like the Palestinian Authority) are dangerous places in which to promote shifts toward democratic governance, because governing institutions are insufficiently capable or authoritative to constrain politics within legitimate bounds. In weak states, where citizens have no faith that the government can or will protect their basic security and welfare, people often fall back on local identities and community-based organizations to protect their interests. In places such as Iraq, Lebanon, and the Palestinian territories, "the weakening and in some cases breakdown of the political infrastructures often leads to a narrowing of identity and social solidarity away from national and towards sectarian, ethnic, and kin-based (however fictive) relations."[3] Politics becomes more localized, and political identity and affinity more polarized. If government weakness extends to an inability to provide basic security, then local political movements (especially those Islamist movements that already employ the rhetoric of resistance) have incentive to cultivate their own military capacity. Local citizens become more supportive of armed militias within their community because they fear that other communities may be doing the same and because they do not view the state as a neutral or effective force for justice.

Elections in such circumstances almost always reflect the localized and polarized politics on the ground, hardening divisions between sectarian or kin-based communities and often handing militant organizations democratic legitimacy as well. Such outcomes bode ill for the development of any democratic system at all. If a democratic system already exists in, or is imposed on, such an environment, it is unlikely to succeed at peacefully accommodating the preferences and demands of these polarized (and armed) communities. This phenomenon is common to weak states across the globe and was on full display in Lebanon, Iraq, and the Palestinian territories.

The first arena of focus was the West Bank and Gaza, where President Bush and his aides consistently stressed the necessity for internal reforms to combat corruption and unify control of security forces under a single civilian command. Bush put these reforms in the context of Palestinian democratization, although their most important effect from an American perspective was to reduce Yasir Arafat's day-to-day influence over Palestinian Authority (PA) policymaking and prevent Western donor money from funding violence by Arafat's Fatah militants against Israel. After Arafat's death, the United States not only endorsed swift elections for a new president of the

Palestinian Authority but also pressed for new parliamentary elections in the territories.

The demand for parliamentary elections came more than three years after the collapse of Israeli-Palestinian negotiations and the onset of near-constant violence between the parties. Israeli military forces were deployed in the midst of Palestinian cities, and Palestinian governance was severely degraded both by destruction of its physical infrastructure and by restrictions on activity imposed by the Israeli military across the territories. Without a government that could guarantee basic security and services, and in the absence of any hope for renewed peace efforts, public support for the militant Hamas movement and its rhetoric of resistance to Israel grew. Hamas's view of the conflict with Israel, in which resistance would liberate territory more effectively than negotiations, was reinforced by Israel's unilateral withdrawal from the Gaza Strip in the fall of 2005. The corrupt, brutal, and inept performance of Fatah leaders both under Arafat and after his demise, and bickering within Fatah, further doomed the party's electoral prospects.

A window of opportunity opened briefly in which a different kind of Israeli-Palestinian diplomacy, and a different American approach, might have diminished Hamas's growing popularity and perhaps led to a different electoral outcome. When Mahmoud Abbas was elected president of the Palestinian Authority in January 2005, he ran on a platform of renewed negotiations with Israel and on rebuilding a clean, effective PA under the principle of "one Authority, one law, one gun." Had he followed up on that promise by collecting weapons from militant groups, including his own Fatah militants, then the PA's governance would have been strengthened and Hamas's claim to public loyalty reduced. Moreover, Israel could have coordinated its withdrawal from the Gaza Strip more closely with the PA, so that Palestinians might have seen it as the fruit of negotiations rather than as a unilateral withdrawal driven by violent resistance. In this situation the Palestinian political dynamic would have been quite different. But neither the Israeli nor the Palestinian political leadership took the steps each might have taken to reduce Hamas's growing influence, and the United States government did not press them to do so. Neither did any of these actors insist on the principle, enshrined in the Oslo accords, that armed movements give up violence before participating in elections (a constraint that would have applied to Fatah as well).

By November 2005 the trend in Palestinian politics was clear enough that some politicians and officials in Ramallah, Jerusalem, and Washington advocated postponing the elections to give Abbas time to regain ground lost to Hamas. Bush, however, held to the notion of open elections as the primary mechanism for democratic advancement in the Arab world. Fatah was able to present unified candidate lists for local district and national elections only in the final days before the balloting. Despite all these missteps, the Fatah party garnered 41 percent of the vote to Hamas's 44 percent—but electoral rules translated that narrow Hamas victory into a sweep of 74 of the 132 available parliamentary seats. The result was an outright victory for a militant Islamist movement committed to the violent destruction of a U.S. ally. Missed opportunities and a misguided focus on democratic process over democratic values produced an outcome with deleterious consequences for the causes of both regional democracy and Arab-Israeli peace.

In Lebanon Bush supported politicians, including former prime minister Rafik Hariri, who were demanding Lebanese independence from Syrian military occupation. After Hariri's assassination in February 2005, the "Beirut Spring" captured Americans' imagination by displaying all the hallmarks of a people-power velvet revolution: multicultural crowds, students sleeping in tents in the city square, sympathetic police helping marchers evade roadblocks. In March 2005 Bush argued that the peaceful demonstrations calling for Syrian withdrawal signaled the cracking of the region's autocratic edifice and the end of Arab rulers' ability to smother popular discontent or co-opt dissenters into submission. He said: "And any who doubt the appeal of freedom in the Middle East can look to Lebanon, where the Lebanese people are demanding a free and independent nation."[4]

But Lebanon's demonstrations, although they surprised and stirred Arab observers, were never likely to be emulated in other Arab capitals, because they were not fundamentally about democracy. The Lebanese opposition labeled the street protests its "independence intifada," not its democracy intifada. The demonstrators demanded the free exercise of Lebanese sovereignty, independent of the influence of their domineering neighbor, Syria. Bush's assessment of the Lebanese situation, however, conflated independence and democracy and pressed for swift parliamentary elections before a new electoral law could be passed to codify the new national consensus in favor of disarming local sectarian militias and in favor of voter choice rather than back-door coalition-building by sectarian elites.[5] The result was an election that ratified existing factional divisions, including a strong showing for Hizballah that gave it several cabinet slots in the new coalition government. Lebanese government decisionmaking was stymied by this fracturing of the political system, and one result was Hizballah's stepped-up military activity against Israel, which provoked the 2006 war.

In Iraq the Bush administration had little choice but to support the establishment of democratic political processes, and ultimately little choice about when to do so. As the military occupier, and having overthrown the dictator, the United States was obliged to develop a successor government, and it was unlikely that America would embrace something other than democracy as the organizing principle for that successor regime. Moreover, the United States initially tried to delay national elections in Iraq, in order to enable pact-making among Iraq's various Shiite, Sunni, and Kurdish factions. But the senior Shiite cleric, Ayatollah Ali al Sistani, pressed for early elections, and the United States could not effectively resist the demand. Unfortunately, the elections took place in an environment of significant sectarian violence, leading voters to favor strong sectarian militias that ran lists in the elections. The result was an Iraqi parliament and government dominated by rival leaders with armed cadres at their disposal and little interest in or incentive for political reconciliation—a recipe for continued instability even should the daily violence decrease.

The fallout was immediate from the Bush administration's decision to press hardest for democracy in areas of the Middle East least capable of sustaining it and to emphasize democratic process over democratic values precisely in places where the process was likeliest simply to coagulate social divisions. In Lebanon Hizballah gained seats in parliament and set up a confrontation with the pro-independence March 14 movement that paralyzed Lebanese governance. In Iraq militia-led Shiite movements swept the first post-Saddam parliamentary elections, crushing new and fragile liberal and cross-sectarian parties and dimming the hopes for a peaceful political reconciliation. In the Palestinian territories parliamentary elections produced an outright victory for the militant Islamist Hamas movement, which vowed to destroy its Israeli neighbor. The U.S. government immediately cut off aid to and political contact with the new Palestinian Authority government, raising charges of hypocrisy across the region.

In attempting democratic change first in places where it was least likely to succeed, the Bush administration made a fundamental misjudgment. It did so because it failed to understand that weak states need functional governance if they are ever to have democratic governance, and it missed this crucial point precisely because it saw these weak places as riper targets, unable to resist American pressure for democracy and unable to retaliate against other American interests. In their desire to avoid confronting autocratic allies on human rights and democracy, Bush and his advisers turned their energies to the most dysfunctional places in the Middle East in the bizarre expectation of easier victory. Clearly, the outcome was a policy failure for Bush's effort at democracy promotion. Just as clearly, it suggests that there is no way to effectively advance democracy in the Middle East without in some manner confronting the strong states of the region, and particularly the United States' autocratic allies, over the issue. As I show in the next chapter, it is possible to do so and to achieve progress at an acceptable price.

Beyond its high-profile diplomacy in Lebanon, Iraq, and Palestine, the Bush administration implemented a host of other measures to advance democracy in the region. These approaches, too, reflected a strong desire to avoid conflicts with autocratic allies, which blunted and diverted the new efforts and ensured the marginality of their effects. Three initiatives in particular are worthy of discussion: the Middle East Free Trade Area (MEFTA) initiative, the Middle East Partnership Initiative (MEPI) and associated democracy assistance funding, and multilateral projects under the auspices of the G8, collectively labeled the Broader Middle East and North Africa (BMENA) Initiative. None of these, however, proved to be an effective tool for advancing democracy in the Arab world, for reasons I discuss next.

Free Trade Promotion

The first of the Bush administration's new programs to advance democratic reform in the Middle East was an initiative to build free trade agreements (FTAs) between the United States and every Middle Eastern country in the coming decade. The MEFTA initiative was designed to increase trade and investment between the United States and the Middle East. It sought to promote the structural, economic, and governance reforms that free international trade and investment require: for example, transparency in government regulation, protection of intellectual property, and the rule of law to enforce contracts. President Bush envisioned a free trade area between the United States and the Middle East built upon these bilateral agreements by

2013.[6] As of 2007, FTAs had been concluded with Jordan, Morocco, Bahrain, and Oman. Negotiations with the United Arab Emirates (UAE) began in 2005, and pre-FTA framework agreements existed with many other Arab states. The U.S. government was also assisting Arab states that had not yet joined the World Trade Organization (WTO) to reach that goal, as an initial step toward improved trade relations with the United States.[7]

Animating the MEFTA initiative was the notion, discussed in the last chapter, that free trade would have benefits for the Middle East beyond reducing poverty and unemployment—that it would help nurture democracy, because trade liberalization and the economic growth it generates would build an independent middle class that would then demand secure property rights, due process of law, and eventually political rights and freedoms from their governments. In its annual reports, Bush's Office of the United States Trade Representative argued that the FTAs it concluded in the Middle East would support political and economic reforms in the partner countries.[8] To underscore the theorized link between economic and political liberalization, the State Department's flagship Middle East democracy assistance program, the Middle East Partnership Initiative, buttressed the MEFTA initiative through technical assistance to Arab governments in meeting their trade obligations and through trade-promotion activities for the private sector.

If the logic of free trade promotion as a means to democratization was what drove MEFTA, then one would have expected a trade policy that focused first on the largest economies in the region and those with the most developed external trade relations. One would also have expected the initiative to advance trade patterns that would maximize benefits for regional economic development. Such a policy would, economists agree, focus on improving trade flows among Arab countries, improving regional integration, and helping the isolated Arab markets coalesce into a single Arab market of 250 million people that could more easily attract and make efficient use of private investment to produce growth and create jobs.

But MEFTA did none of these things. Instead of encouraging regional economic integration, MEFTA hampered it by building a series of exclusive, bilateral agreements between the United States and individual Arab countries. The negative effect on regional integration was visible in the Gulf Cooperation Council, where a decade of efforts to remove internal customs and tariff barriers and move toward a unified currency were disrupted by the requirements FTAs with the United States imposed on Oman and Bahrain.[9] Moreover, the American approach of negotiating country-by-country agreements promoted—by design, according to current and former trade officials—a competitive dynamic between Arab states, provoking a race to get preferential access to the massive American market.

So there was from the beginning good reason to doubt the effectiveness of the Bush administration's use of free trade agreements as a democratizing tool. But when one takes a closer look at the assumption about the democratizing effect of economic reform, there is even more reason for skepticism. The easy availability of income from oil and other sources has long relieved many Arab regimes of the necessity of extracting taxes from citizens and therefore from giving in to citizens' political demands in exchange. Given the complication that oil rents pose to the assumed relationship between economic and political freedom, it is notable that three of the first five American FTA efforts in the region involved relatively small oil-producing states: Bahrain, Oman, and the UAE. Negotiations with these countries were relatively straightforward because the trade volumes were small and the local economies fairly one-dimensional. Negotiations with Bahrain required a mere four months, and those with Oman only seven.[10] Freer trade relations with these states did not, by and large, threaten American industries with new competition, making congressional approval easier to obtain.

The small Persian Gulf states were eager to jump on the MEFTA bandwagon precisely because FTAs did not by and large threaten their domestic power relations. Arab regimes with larger, more diverse economies rely on more complex networks of preferential economic relations to support their rule and worry more about lost jobs and other destabilizing effects of freer trade. They have therefore been more reluctant to embrace the reforms that an FTA entails. The United States and Egypt, for example, despite long-standing and well-developed trade relations, have struggled to keep their Trade and Investment Framework Agreement (TIFA) on track through years of contentious discussions. Trade negotiations between Egypt and the United States are also complicated by competition between the two states' large and politically important cotton and textile producers. Because of such domestic concerns and Egypt's peripatetic approach to economic reform, and more recently because of its poor human rights record, the United States government has been unwilling to open talks on a free trade agreement.

These difficulties point to the limits of MEFTA as a strategy to promote regional reform: it works to support liberalization only in states that have already chosen to embrace liberalization. Where that commitment to liberalizing reform is evident, free-trade-related policy changes may have some positive effect on governance. For example, requiring public disclosure of regulatory changes may give indigenous labor and environmental NGOs better information and thus a better chance to influence policy. Competitive bidding for government contracting may reduce corruption and help small businesses compete against regime-favored business elites. The FTAs signed under Bush included provisions on labor standards, government transparency, and other issues that might, over time, become useful tools for reformers. Bahrain, for example, has now legalized labor unions, as required by its FTA.

If the commitment to liberal reform is not already present in Arab regimes, however, then these technical aspects of FTAs are unlikely to do the job alone. The MEFTA initiative failed to engage the larger economies of the region and has not demonstrated a capacity to increase local employment or build up an independent, export-oriented private sector. As a result, its effects on regional democratization are likely to be limited.

Democracy Assistance Funding

The best-known element of Bush's Freedom Agenda was a new mechanism for the delivery of American assistance to the Middle East, designed to promote reform in economics, politics, and education by linking assistance closely to diplomacy and by providing help directly to Arab citizens and citizen associations. The Middle East Partnership Initiative was the brainchild of Elizabeth Cheney, then deputy assistant secretary of state for Near Eastern affairs (and daughter of the vice president). Launched in December 2002 with $29 million in reallocated State Department funds, the initiative, known as MEPI, was formulated as the flagship for the new American approach to the region, which emphasized development of long-term alliances with the peoples of the Middle East rather than with specific ruling regimes. MEPI wielded budgetary and bureaucratic resources that were meant to realign U.S. diplomacy and assistance in the Middle East in the direction of democracy promotion. An examination of MEPI thus tells a broader story about the Bush administration's progress toward ending the exception made for the Middle East in U.S. democracy promotion policy and of the obstacles and dangers that threaten to undermine or cut short this bold policy change.

MEPI's founders conceived the program to be a major departure from traditional U.S. assistance in the Middle East. Instead of large-scale, long-term development projects like those supported by the U.S. Agency for International Development (USAID), MEPI provided smaller grants for programs of two years' duration or less. MEPI sought both effect and legitimacy by addressing the reform priorities identified by Arab scholars in the 2002 UN Arab Human Development Report. That report identified three deficits hindering developmental progress in the Arab world: deficits in political and economic freedom, in knowledge, and in women's empowerment. MEPI was thus divided into four pillars: political reform, economic reform, educational reform, and women's empowerment. From its inception in December 2002 through 2007 MEPI received more than $500 million in congressionally appropriated funds.[11] In addition to spending its own money, the MEPI office—thanks to bureaucratic battles waged by Elizabeth Cheney—won a role in determining the allocation of the USAID's funds for democracy and governance in the Middle East and became a hub for interagency discussion of policy under the Freedom Agenda.

Two key goals of MEPI were to build partnerships with nongovernmental Middle Eastern groups and local citizens and to encourage links among reformers across Middle Eastern countries. Inherent in this approach was a judgment that Arab governments had insufficiently recognized their looming demographic and economic challenges or embraced the need for political, economic, and social reform. Instead, the thinking went, they would need to be goaded toward change by a combination of independent American assistance and local grassroots activism.

In its first two years of operation MEPI had trouble finding suitable places to spend its relatively large appropriations for civil-society-based democracy promotion.[12] Its activities suffered early on from perceptions among some career U.S. officials that the very notion of independently funding pro-reform activities presented a conflict of interest for the United States government. With no field staff of its own and little understanding of the Arab civil society landscape, MEPI in its first two years relied heavily on local U.S. embassy staff and even Arab governments themselves to suggest new programs, recommend grantees, and nominate participants in regional programs. In practice that meant that MEPI's intent to further the growth of an independent civic sector in Arab states was blunted by the direction of MEPI funds toward programs favored by host governments, such as girls' literacy, and toward "benign" recipients, including regime-sponsored NGOs.

In the end, MEPI's first two years of funding went in large part to programs that were unlikely to have much effect on regional democratization. Indeed, despite MEPI's intention to encourage the growth and activity of the Arab civic sector, much of its early funding was directed instead toward technical assistance to government agencies and officials. More than 70 percent of its first $103 million in grants went to programs that either directly benefited Arab government agencies (in activities ranging from translating documents to computerizing schools) or provided training programs and seminars for Arab government officials (including ministry bureaucrats, parliamentarians, and judges).[13] Although MEPI improved its record of nongovernmental funding in later years, programs that actually supported either the capacities or the actual activities of Arab civic groups always represented a small portion of its overall funding.

This failure to focus funds on the organizations and activities that MEPI's founders intended to champion was not mainly the consequence of ignorance or ineptitude. The major barrier to effective U.S. support for Arab civil society was (and is) the hostility of autocratic Arab governments to any greater independence or activism in the nongovernmental sector. To enable Arab activists to organize, gain public support, and build effective challenges both to their governments and to the Islamist monopoly of the opposition ground, the U.S. government must go beyond funding for civic groups to frontally address with Arab governments the imperative for improved freedom of association. The right of civic activists to organize and operate is a fundamental prerequisite if training them is to have any effect. Assistance programs such as MEPI must be accompanied by firm diplomatic support for political freedoms if they are to be effective.

As government budgets grew tight (in light of tax cuts and the expense of the war in Iraq, congressional appropriators grew first skeptical of MEPI's goals and then, with the advent of the Democratic-led 110th Congress, hostile. In this environment MEPI felt increasing pressure to "spend out" its appropriation and to generate visible or quantifiable results in order to justify new annual requests. Consequently, the initiative devoted increasing shares of its funding to programs that drew participants from across the region into short-term training seminars or exchange visits (three days to three weeks) and thus generated a large number of "MEPI alumni" in a relatively short time. Between fiscal years 2002 and 2006, fully 51 percent of MEPI's programs were training and exchange programs. After these programs were over, the participants were sent home, presumably to implement what they had learned about press freedom, campaign tactics, and the like. In the unforgiving environment most of these MEPI alumni faced, however, those lessons were of limited application.

MEPI grants also performed a variety of functions that were directly related not to democracy promotion but to the broader goal of reform. These programs ran the gamut from the mundane to the visionary. For example, MEPI helped the trade ministries of the Arab states in the Persian Gulf to adapt to their obligations under the WTO and other global trading rules. The initiative also translated children's stories into Arabic to build classroom libraries and brought Arab businesswomen to the United States for internships with major American companies. Although these projects individually presented worthy opportunities to improve the lives of Arab men, women, and children, the sheer diversity of audiences and issues addressed by the programs inevitably limited both the scope and the longevity of their effects. Even if MEPI's spending on such programs were increased by an order of magnitude, it would not bring democracy to a single country.

Trends in MEPI activities over time reveal a clear shift away from the program's intended focus on independent support for local Arab pro-reform efforts and toward bilateral and multilateral efforts to promote gradual liberalization. In 2002 less than 10 percent of MEPI funds was spent on external commitments such as support for the MEFTA initiative, whereas by fiscal year 2006 the proportion was well over 30 percent (figure 5-1). The increasing external demands placed on MEPI's budget and the shrinking portion of the budget left for support of MEPI program priorities suggest that the administration grew increasingly uncomfortable with the more confrontational aspects of MEPI's work and preferred to channel funds to projects that grew out of bilateral agreements with Arab governments (trade promotion and trade-related technical assistance) or were multilateral and consensual (such as funding for BMENA initiatives).

Figure 5-1. *Percentage of MEPI Funds Devoted to MEFTA and BMENA Support*

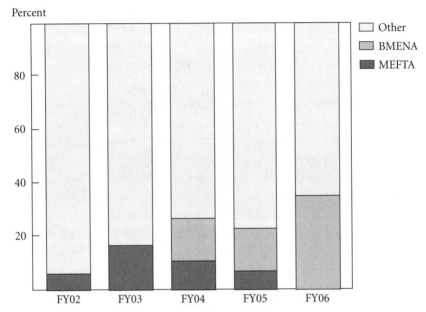

Source: Author's calculations using data from http://mepi.state.gov, http://bmena.state.gov, and Department of State Congressional Notifications, FY02–FY06.

Moreover, the bureaucratic imperatives to avoid confrontation with Arab governments and justify program funding to Congress has sometimes led MEPI to emphasize publicity-friendly projects over low-profile but longer-term efforts to build Arab reform movements. A sobering story of what MEPI did wrong in this regard emerged from a MEPI-sponsored "Gulf Regional Campaign School" held in Qatar in February 2004. Unsatisfied with gathering several dozen women activists to discuss running for political office, MEPI wanted to conclude the seminar with a press conference to advertise its success. But when the Arab participants drafted a final communiqué for the press conference that included criticisms of U.S. policy toward the Israeli-Palestinian conflict, a MEPI representative compelled a last-minute change in the schedule, ensuring that the women were not in attendance at the right time to present their communiqué.

At its worst, the conflict-of-interests problem led State Department officials to design programs not merely to appear benign to Arab governments but actively to bolster U.S.-Arab bilateral ties and serve the goal of U.S. public diplomacy, at the expense of advancing meaningful reform in any sector. A primary example of this distortion of MEPI's work was the U.S.–Middle East Partnership for Breast Cancer Awareness and Research. This project focused MEPI funds and programming effort on promoting awareness and treatment of breast cancer among women in Saudi Arabia; Jordan and the United Arab Emirates later joined the project as well. The rationale provided by State Department officials was that women in Saudi Arabia and other conservative gulf societies were either too conservative or too confined to be able to organize around social and political issues, but breast cancer and health care were "safe" subjects for women's dialogue and activism. Therefore, building citizen networks around breast cancer awareness would facilitate the organizational capacity and civic engagement of Saudi and other gulf women.[14]

This was, to begin with, a misreading of the environment in the Arab gulf states. Saudi women are among the most educated in the Arab world, and women outnumber men at many gulf Arab universities. An increasing number become medical doctors, both because of the educational subsidies available and the high demand for female doctors to care for female patients. Saudi women do not lack interest or engagement in civic affairs and do not suffer from any evident incapacity to organize. As early as 1990 a group of Saudi women successfully organized a one-day demonstration in Riyadh, taking the wheels of automobiles to protest the government's driving ban for women. In 2005 two women became the first-ever elected women in the country when they won seats on the Jeddah Chamber of Commerce with a great number of male votes.[15] At the same time MEPI was launching its breast cancer initiative, Saudi women columnists in national newspapers were arguing for liberal reforms and criticizing clerics and others who promoted outdated views of the relationship between husband and wife.[16] Clearly, Saudi women were neither incapable of making demands on the state nor uninterested in mobilizing public support for their views.

But MEPI officials did not reach out to these brave women. Instead, they gave priority to a project that had the full approval of the Saudi government and was engineered to produce feel-good press coverage. First Lady Laura Bush flew to the gulf to celebrate the breast cancer effort as a means to "build lasting friendships between our countries."[17] Only fierce lobbying by mid-level MEPI staffers compelled the organizers of the first lady's breast cancer tour to give a few hours of her schedule to visits with participants in other MEPI programs on English literacy and women's leadership. The conflict-of-interests problem, in this instance, led to a hijacking of the flagship U.S. democracy assistance program on behalf of public diplomacy aims.

Even when the Bush administration targeted the right issues, it largely failed to match its external efforts with the demands being raised by reformers in Arab states and to coordinate its assistance programs for civil society with its diplomatic agenda. Despite being deliberately placed in the Near East Affairs Bureau, MEPI was often unable to mobilize American diplomacy on behalf of greater freedom of association in Arab states or on behalf of the more specific goals being sought by MEPI-supported Arab NGOs. The rationale for situating MEPI in the State Department's regional bureau was that from there its reform goals could be more easily integrated into America's ongoing diplomatic dialogue with Arab states. Even at MEPI's budgetary and bureaucratic zenith, however, its leaders had only limited success in getting its views on democracy promotion heard in interagency meetings or getting talking points about democracy and human rights on the agendas for U.S. government meetings with senior Arab officials.

As a result, the president's public rhetoric was not always matched by private messages. President Bush commendably exhorted Tunisian president Zine El Abidine Ben Ali during a 2004 White House visit to allow a free press, but the administration did not follow up on the issue, even when Tunisia's repressive press record became an international issue, with either programming or public statements, ahead of a UN meeting Tunisia hosted the following year. Also in 2004, several Saudi journalists lost their jobs or their columns after they questioned the influence of extremist clerics in politics and the exclusion of women from public life. No exhortations on their behalf were issued from a Washington podium. When the United States fails to speak up for those who challenge the system, it reduces the incentive for others to try—and activists who might like to take the U.S. president's words seriously and look to America for support feel betrayed.

To be effective, U.S. democracy assistance must be designed in a way that will relieve the constant pressure MEPI felt from embassy staff and Washington officials to favor short-term, consensual projects on education and trade in order to avoid confrontations with Arab governments. Empowering local actors and facilitating local coalition-building often means avoiding the spotlight and minimizing the American imprint on projects supported by U.S. government assistance. Indeed, some of the MEPI programs that most effectively built local civil society and forged links among local democracy activists were not designed or run from Washington at all but were bottom-up programs generated through dialogue between local activists, local U.S. embassy personnel, and MEPI's two regional offices. Because these grants were small and local, they operated under the radar of budget hawks and congressional critics. Because they had been developed in consultation with local U.S. embassy officials, the embassies were more likely to defend them should they raise hackles in bilateral relations.

Ultimately, resisting the short-term exigencies of the Washington funding and policymaking process requires that the Middle East Partnership Initiative, or its successor, identify concrete milestones and opportunities for interim progress on long-term issues such as the advancement of political liberties. If democracy promotion in the Middle East is a long, difficult process that will not produce its real fruits in the short term, then funding and programming must reflect this long-term approach while developing short-term markers of progress, rather than bowing to short-term imperatives with programs that subvert long-term goals. Congressional appropriators and executive-branch overseers must likewise respect and support a long-term strategy.

In addition, MEPI's limited effects demonstrate the importance of putting diplomacy front and center in a democracy-promotion effort. There is simply no substitute for direct engagement with local governments, especially over the constraints they place on basic political freedoms—constraints that can stymie even the most cutting-edge democracy assistance funding. Even a democracy-promotion strategy that relies on cultivating mass civil disobedience to a restrictive autocratic regime—the Czechoslovakia model, one might call it—is premised on the idea that there are limits to a regime's willingness to repress dissent. Those limits are frequently calibrated with reference to international and, most important, American opinion. American silence on basic political rights and freedoms is not a form of neutrality; rather, it speaks volumes to dictators about what they can get away with in dealing with their own citizens and to local democratic activists about what they risk when they challenge governmental authority.

Multilateral Efforts

In June 2004 the United States government hosted the Sea Island summit of the Group of Eight major industrialized states and made Middle East democracy its signature issue. The Broader Middle East and North Africa Initiative, adopted by the G8 at that meeting, cemented a consensus among Western states that continued political stagnation in the Arab Middle East threatened the peace and stability of that region as well as the security of Western states. The BMENA statement of principles committed G8 states to the goal of democratic change. The initiative's limited means do not match this goal. The firm desire among G8 governments to work "in partnership" with Arab governments on reform led them to soft-pedal the actual democracy-promotion content of the BMENA Initiative.

The cornerstone of the BMENA Initiative is the Forum for the Future, an annual meeting of governments and business and civil society groups from the G8 and the Middle East. By 2006 Western governments had succeeded in corralling all the Arab governments to show up at the Forum for the Future, but at the price of limiting NGO participation and watering down the agenda to emphasize economic issues more than democracy. The host of the 2005 forum, Bahrain, used executive powers to forbid public marches during the meeting, creating a bizarre contrast between the values purportedly embraced by the conference delegates and those being enforced in the street. The Egyptian government also managed to scuttle, for a period of time, what would have been the forum's only substantive product, a draft declaration that would have called on Arab states to allow greater scope of action for local NGOs.[18] In 2007 the United States was distracted by efforts to rejuvenate Israeli-Palestinian peace talks, and no Forum was held—proving that, in the end, the Forum had no momentum beyond that lent by Washington.

In addition, BMENA comprises several small, multilateral projects designed mainly to assist the development of private enterprise in the Middle East and to promote literacy and job training. But there are no governance criteria, even informal, for Arab state participation in these projects. The result is that Arab states are offered the West's help in implementing the economic reforms they largely want while they ignore Western pressures for the political reforms they do not want.

Most notably, BMENA launched a Foundation for the Future, which was meant to pool international funds to support Arab nongovernmental democratization efforts. This project was intended to have an independent, nongovernmental board of directors to ensure freedom of action in making grants to local NGOs. The United States devoted a significant portion of MEPI's 2006 budget, $35 million, to underwriting the foundation's endowment. But in its eagerness to get Arab government acquiescence for the project and at least symbolic amounts of Arab government funding, the United States agreed to give Arab government donors a voice in selecting the board's membership and to have the foundation register as an NGO under the laws of the country in which it would operate, Jordan. The net effect was to make the foundation beholden to the very governments it was meant to challenge and to constrain its freedom of action.

In the end BMENA fell prey to the ideal of "partnership" between Arab and Western governments in the pursuit of reform. American (and European) interests in Arab reform dictate far-reaching goals that diverge from the path chosen by most of the G8's regional allies. The challenge for the United States and the West, then, is to discover how to shift Arab regimes' comfort with the choices they have made and to push them, however marginally, beyond where they want right now to go.

Case Study: Egypt's 2005 Elections

It should be clear from the preceding discussion that any effective democracy promotion policy must combine bottom-up assistance for pro-democracy civic groups with top-down diplomacy that presses governments to allow greater scope for public debate of political issues. The American approach to Egypt's 2005 presidential and parliamentary elections shows, more clearly than any other example, how the fear of Islamist gains and the concern over alienating a strategic ally handicapped the United States from managing this feat, even given President Bush's firm commitment to promoting democracy in the Arab world.

As Egypt looked toward 2005, the first year in many in which presidential and parliamentary balloting would coincide, the country was at a moment of decision. Hosni Mubarak, president since Sadat's assassination in 1981, had governed under a state of emergency and been reelected four times in a noncompetitive, yes-or-no referendum. At seventy-six years of age Mubarak still refused to appoint a vice president—the government official who constitutionally would succeed him if he died in office—or otherwise clarify plans for government in his absence. In the year leading up to the elections U.S. government officials spoke publicly about democracy in Egypt but garbled its message in private. When Mubarak visited President Bush's Crawford, Texas, ranch in March 2004, working-level staff on both sides negotiated the leaders' prepared statements to the press and included landmark references to reform and democracy. But in their one-on-one meeting, Bush apparently did not raise the issue of Egyptian political reform at all, fixating instead on Israel's announced plan to withdraw from the Gaza Strip. With Mubarak's eye on his fifth presidential referendum, Bush's omission no doubt sent a powerful message.

Eventually, however, Bush's pro-democracy rhetoric had an effect in Cairo, especially after Bush took a high-profile stance in 2003 on behalf of Saad Eddin Ibrahim, a democracy activist and dual U.S.-Egyptian citizen imprisoned on trumped-up charges after distributing a documentary about voting fraud in the 2000 elections.[19] The Bush administration's diplomatic efforts with other Arab states embarrassed Egypt into going along first with an Arab League statement on democracy in March 2004 and then with the G8's convening of the Forum for the Future, in which Arab governments were compelled to listen to civil society and business activists make public demands for political and economic reform. As 2005 approached, local democracy activists began a series of weekly protests in the Egyptian capital under the simple slogan "Enough!" asking voters to say no to Mubarak in the upcoming referendum. A new liberal party called al-Ghad won legal status in the courts after Mubarak's government denied it registration.

Mubarak responded by arresting al-Ghad's leader, Ayman Nour, on charges of forgery and by using force against the demonstrators. But he also announced, in a stunning surprise, that he would sponsor constitutional amendments to enable a competitive presidential ballot instead of the usual plebiscite. The parliament, overwhelmingly dominated by the ruling National Democratic Party, quickly passed constitutional changes that allowed open competition for all legal parties in this first race, but it set severe restrictions on ballot access for future elections. A public referendum on the changes was scheduled for just a week after parliamentary voting finished. Additional legislation passed that summer confirmed severe penalties for journalists found guilty of libel or defamation, and strengthened the government's ability to interfere with and even shut down political parties.

Throughout this rushed legislative process the U.S. government abstained from making specific judgments about the changes under way, instead praising the fact of change and expressing some expectations about the elections, particularly about the importance of international monitors and the need for open media access for all candidates. Secretary Rice, in perhaps the boldest moment of the Freedom Agenda's course, made a public speech in Cairo emphasizing these demands and declaring that "for sixty years, my country, the United States, pursued stability at the expense of democracy in this region here in the Middle East—and we achieved neither. Now we are taking a different course. We are supporting the democratic aspirations of all people."[20] Her high-profile statements, however, failed to take note of the restrictions placed on the presidential competition or of the retrograde changes made under the guise of "reform" to laws affecting the press and political parties.

The net effect of Mubarak's hurried legal changes was to create an electoral process that was formally competitive but that tightened restrictions on parties, press, and ballot access in a way that kept the electoral outcome closely controlled. The constraints on the basic political freedoms of speech and association easily trumped the formally competitive electoral process. Mubarak successfully resisted Bush's demand for international monitors on sovereignty grounds, but public and international pressure and rulings by a few brave judges (later punished by the government-controlled judges' authority) compelled him to allow domestic citizen monitors. Belatedly, in the summer of 2005, USAID offered funds to U.S.-based NGOs to support local efforts including monitoring. Little programming was under way by the time balloting began in the fall.

In the presidential election, Mubarak won 88.6 percent of the vote, but voter turnout was only 22.9 percent. Parliamentary voting took place in three rounds, with state repression and voter intimidation escalating as the balloting progressed and the opposition's gains became clearer. In the end, the Muslim Brotherhood's candidates took 20 percent of the parliament's 454 seats, but their lack of legal party status prevented them from taking on the formal role of parliamentary opposition.

Despite the American funding supporting the domestic monitors, for weeks the State Department refused to respond to the citizen monitors' reports of fraud and news accounts of security services preventing voters from reaching the polls. Only after the final round of voting was completed did the State Department issue a relatively mild statement of concern. Indeed, the post-election period saw a sharp decline in American attention to or expressions of concern over Egyptian political development. In contrast to Rice's June 2005 landmark speech in Cairo, official American visits in 2006 and 2007 were focused on Iraq, Iran, and Israel, with virtually no public American expressions of support for reform. Analysts and observers explained the shift in the diplomatic discourse from Washington as reflecting the need for Arab help in dealing with chaos in Iraq and a cooled enthusiasm for Arab democracy in the light of gains by Islamist movements in Egypt and the Palestinian territories.[21] In practice, then, the conduct of American diplomacy, despite Bush's rhetoric, endorsed gradual liberalization, tacitly approving Mubarak's steps to place democratic window dressing on his authoritarianism and to leave the only constitutional means for his succession unavailable by refusing to appoint a vice president.

The mistakes made by the Bush administration in Egypt—fixating on political processes while ignoring the repressive environment in which they took place, embracing any regime-led change as positive, and heralding elections even when their results were eminently predictable and irrelevant to the prospects for freedom—have been repeated across the region in similar, though less extreme cases in Yemen, Jordan, Morocco, and Bahrain. The Egyptian case, like these others, illustrates another deep flaw in the strategy of gradualist liberalization and highlights the dangers it carries for the United States. If a guided liberalization undertaken with American support comes to be perceived by citizens as a minimalist sham, or if it is quickly reversed in the wake of public demands for even more liberalization, then the United States becomes as much associated with the subsequent repression and reversal as it might have been with the prior opening. Today, as Egyptian liberal bloggers, journalists, and politicians feel the weight of an official crackdown, they rue that they ever believed enough in America's rhetoric to stick their necks out for democratic reform.

After the September 11 attacks, the Bush administration embraced, in principle, the need for American policy to support comprehensive and far-reaching reforms in Arab politics, economics, and society—reforms that included meaningful democratization. In bold language President Bush declared an end to "sixty years of excusing and accommodating the lack of freedom in the Middle East."[22] But in practice the Bush administration failed to live up to its commitments. Its efforts were both insufficiently ambitious and badly designed. Despite his radical reinterpretation of American imperatives in the Middle East, Bush's policy generally supported regime-led liberalization that would never yield full democracy and has already served to entrench Islamist movements and crowd out liberals and other alternative voices. Moreover, even where the Bush administration created sharper-edged, pro-democracy policy tools such as MEPI, their results were blunted by the failure to effectively marry them to robust American diplomacy.

The Freedom Agenda fell so far short of Bush's rhetoric because of the enduring ambivalence of American attitudes toward democracy in this troubled part of the world. The dual operation of the Algeria problem and the worry that democracy promotion will sacrifice U.S.-Arab strategic cooperation continue to hold policymakers in thrall and prevent effective steps to cope with the already-upon-us reality of Arab political change. In trying to navigate these two dilemmas, the Bush administration built a policy that sounded revolutionary but settled into a timid, ultimately hapless pattern. The United States provides funds to Arab civil society activists but does not consistently support them when their activities bring down the wrath of their governments. American democracy implementers exhort judges and journalists to take up the independent roles they should play in a democratic society, but American officials do not defend the efforts of these brave pioneers when their activism lands them in jail. American policy insists that electoral mandates are the gold standard of political legitimacy, but when the younger son of Egypt's long-time president, who has been elected to no public office, visits Washington, he is received at the White House by the vice president, with a drop-by greeting from the president of the United States.[23]

With this record, it is no wonder that America's purported democracy drive in the Middle East lacks credibility either with democracy advocates or, more seriously, with Arab autocrats. Instead, these cynical rulers rely on the United States' preoccupation with Iraq and the American electoral calendar. They feel confident that when a new U.S. president takes office, they will go back to business as usual with the White House.

CHAPTER SIX

Overcoming Ambivalence

T HE BUSH ADMINISTRATION's efforts to advance democracy in the Middle East fell prey to a deep-seated ambivalence among America's foreign policy elites and officials regarding the causes and consequences of democratization in the Arab world. The concern that Arab democratization might simply enshrine anti-American, radically religious regimes and that democratization might come to the Middle East only at the price of U.S.-Arab strategic cooperation led policymakers to blunt the edges of the Freedom Agenda regularly and at every level of officialdom. It is possible that such a half-hearted, inconsistent policy will in the long term have a more detrimental effect than a simple hands-off approach. Clearly, the failures of the Freedom Agenda since it was announced in 2003 have magnified the credibility gap faced by the United States in advocating democracy in this region.

Can these failings be corrected? America's attitude toward political reform in the Arab world will have profound consequences for the region's future whether or not the United States engages directly in democracy assistance efforts. Can America's role in the struggles to redefine Arab politics now taking place across the region be a constructive one? The United States faces two primary challenges in formulating a more effective and sustainable democracy promotion policy than Bush's Freedom Agenda. It must confront the problem of its conflicting interests in the region, and it must tackle the legacy of Algeria. In this chapter I focus on the first of these daunting problems, and in the next chapter, on the second.

A policy designed to promote democracy while taking account of other American interests in the Middle East is necessarily a balancing act, one that will sometimes seem hypocritical and inconsistent. Some basic principles, however, can be articulated.

First, any strategy for the United States in promoting democratic change must, in most Arab states, be an *engagement* strategy. It would be unwise for the United States to foment popular revolutions in Arab states—even if it could—because the likely leaders of those revolutions would be neither liberal-democratic in outlook nor pro-American in attitude. Similarly, it would be unwise to align America's power wholly with dissident liberal politicians, who are marginal, against regimes with which the United States has worked and must continue to work on other important issues. Thus any American strategy on reform must be centered on its most significant regional relationships: those with the regimes now in power.

America's engagement strategy must work to alter the environments within which regime leaders make their decisions about what types of reform to pursue and on what timetable. The United States must work to maximize the discomfort that leaders associate with the status quo and also to maximize the payoff to them for moving toward more liberal politics, economies, and societies. The American strategy cannot be consistent across all countries and at all times; priorities must adjust both to local circumstances and to the mix of U.S. interests at play in a given country. Pursuing comprehensive reform does not mean pursuing all good things at once, nor does it mean applauding whatever priorities and programs Arab leaders may choose to embrace while ignoring their failures of leadership. Because choices will be required between the pursuit of reform, even narrowly defined, and other policy goals, America's priorities must be held clearly in mind.

Yet the United States' goal for the Arab Middle East must be *comprehensive* reform. American strategy must be directed explicitly toward the goal of democracy, not merely toward regime-guided, limited liberalization, which is the chosen strategy of most Arab regimes today. The Bush administration largely acquiesced in these liberalization strategies and added only a marginal element of independent pro-democracy assistance that could not hope to overcome the pro-regime attitude underlying most of its diplomacy in the region. America needs to push for something more ambitious. Critically, its interest in Arab reform cannot be isolated to a single sphere of politics, economics, or society. The challenges facing the region demand far-reaching changes. These political, economic, and social problems reinforce one another and can be effectively addressed only through similarly interlinked political, economic, and social reforms. Yet democratic rights and freedoms are essential to this process, for reasons I will relate.

Most important, while advocating reform in all these spheres, the strategy must prioritize which countries of the Arab world should feel the most focused American attention on behalf of democracy, as well as which among the various issues and arenas within which reform can take place should earn the greatest American effort.

Within the Arab world, the Bush administration's error of pressing hardest on the weakest states must be repaired. The most hopeful places in the region for transitions to democracy are countries with strong governments that have already overcome or have not had to face the challenges of militant Islamism, endemic violence, and ethnic divisions that plague Iraq, Lebanon, and Palestine. America must also, in setting priorities, take account of its own credibility deficit: it must pay closest attention to states with which it has the closest relations if it wishes to be taken seriously by the regimes and the peoples of the region.

Putting Freedom First

In building a new strategy to promote reform in the Arab world, the United States can and should distinguish between more urgent objectives and those that can be achieved only more gradually, and it should set reform priorities with an eye to reducing the risks of a pro-reform policy to other U.S. interests. The highest-priority goal toward which American diplomatic, financial, and other policy tools should be deployed is the expansion of *basic political freedoms*: freedom of expression (including media freedom), freedom of assembly, and freedom of association. In other words, when U.S. officials consider which elements of reform are worth paying a price for, they should weigh the expansion of political freedoms more heavily than procedural improvements in, say, voting or the administration of justice.

A "freedoms first" approach offers three distinct benefits. First, the protection and enhancement of basic political freedoms is the surest pathway to steady progress in democratization and the best insurance against back-sliding into authoritarianism. When citizens have the ability to organize themselves and voice their grievances, they can make public demands on government and hold leaders publicly accountable for the promises they make. When citizens can voice dissent and reveal abuses, they can mobilize local and international support for their demands for redress. In cases from Burma to Belarus, determined domestic activists have found ways to let the world know of their situation and to bring added international pressure to bear on their governments. Once governments begin to improve the availability of political rights, those very rights can be used to constrain government power and to protect and expand the zone of freedom within that society.

Second, the exercise of basic political freedoms will help address the Algeria problem by enabling a reduction over time in the monopoly of Islamist movements over the political opposition. I detail this process in chapter seven, but the core argument is that Islamists' privileged position in the opposition is a result of an artificially constrained political marketplace, a duopoly of regimes and undifferentiated Islamists. Freedom of press, speech, and association will not only allow non-Islamist political move-ments to emerge, advertise, and build support but also encourage diversifi-cation within the broad stream of political Islam, creating greater clarity and competition between Islamist groups and reducing the salience of Islamism as a catchall category for political dissent. Public support for Islamists will become differentiated and will likely shrink overall, and the Algeria scenario will become increasingly unlikely.

Third, the voice given to citizens by the extension of basic political free-doms will ensure that external pressure never outstrips internal demands for change. In South Korea, the Philippines, and Chile, one key to the suc-cess of American interventions on behalf of democracy was the existence and activism of a credible, grassroots domestic democracy movement. Without the existence of such movements, it is hard indeed for the United States to advocate effectively for change. But today's Arab world does not display mass-based movements for democracy, and questions are rife in U.S. policy circles about whether American support for more marginal political movements and political leaders is helpful or hurtful to their prospects for broader mobilization. Whether American assistance is a boon or, as some would have it, a "kiss of death" for local democracy activists is a judgment best made by the activists themselves. Without an opportunity to speak freely, these movements and leaders cannot weigh in on this crucial question of how the United States can best support their cause.

A focus on basic freedoms was the biggest missing piece in the Bush administration's strategy. In case after case the U.S. government raised the issue of reform in its dialogues with Arab regimes but failed to concentrate on the right questions at the right time (and finally began to fail to speak up at all). When Egypt's ruling party was harassing opposition candidates and preparing constitutional amendments that would severely restrict ballot access in future presidential elections, the United States was asking for international monitoring on election day (it also did press for freer press coverage of the campaign). After the elections were over, the U.S. government did not pay close attention while Mubarak rammed through constitutional changes far worse than those in 2005—changes that made permanent the security services' emergency powers.

The power of basic political freedoms is that they make other forms of democratic progress possible by creating space for Arab citizens and reform-minded officials to do what they already want to do, giving them greater opportunities to act on their own and to build coalitions on behalf of change. In such an environment, local activists can raise their own demands, and external actors such as the United States can more easily line up behind them. Governments then face a combination of internal and external pressures, both exerted in the same direction. Political freedoms enable citizens to influence the shape of change even without a vote and also help prevent autocratic governments from reneging on reforms without facing a backlash. If a leader has made a commitment to, say, a constitutional reform, civic groups can organize to educate the public on the issue, lay out expectations, and build demand. Media can publicly shame leaders who fail to follow through, and citizens can gather to protest if the reform is abandoned. All these things, so basic to politics in a consolidated democracy, are not reliable options in the Arab world today.

Advocating a freedoms-first approach does not mean that the United States should embrace and try to implement a strategy for Arab reform that sequences political reforms by putting elections at the end of a long process of political liberalization—the approach advocated by Fareed Zakaria in *The Future of Freedom*.[1] The United States, after all, does not have the ability to enforce such an approach, and most Arab states already hold regular elections, flawed and fixed though they may be in some cases. Whatever political liberalization occurs will do so in the context of preexisting structures created by autocrats, structures that may already include elections and other procedural elements of democracy.

A freedoms-first approach means that even if sham elections are already a regular feature of a given state's politics, improved freedom of speech, press, and assembly will enable citizens to discuss and debate the significance of their electoral process and express their desires for a more meaningful one. And if citizens voting in sham elections feel freer to register protest votes, then that, too, can increase pressure on government and opposition alike to come up with substantive solutions to the problems voters face. The abysmal turnout in the 2007 Moroccan parliamentary election, for example, should have provoked introspection among Morocco's political elites, but a pre-election crackdown on press freedom intimidated journalists from openly discussing the reasons voters abandoned the political process. If the king is ever to be expected to acknowledge the need for reforms meaningful enough to engage citizen participation in politics, the quality of public discussion must improve—and press freedom will be essential to that process.

What does this mean in practice? It means that the United States must press Arab regimes to reform their *politics,* not just their political *processes.* In Egypt in 2005, for example, America's two core demands regarding the revised elections were increased press freedom to cover candidates and campaigns and international monitoring of the vote itself. A focus on basic political freedoms would have kept the emphasis on press freedom and deemed international monitoring a less important issue than constraints on party registration and ballot access. Freedom of association, after all, is a crucial ingredient to producing opposition parties that can mount effective challenges to the Muslim Brotherhood's monopoly on dissent and win the allegiance of moderate voters and business leaders who currently ally with the ruling party out of fear of the alternative. In Egypt local civic groups and judges were already mobilized to provide citizen monitoring on election day in a bid to reduce fraud—indeed, some of the NGOs received American assistance to do so. In this case the emphasis on international monitoring was a distraction; U.S. leverage would have been better spent working to make the ballot more meaningful by pressing for the legalization of several new parties whose bids for licenses had been denied and by pushing back against the regime's plan to let only well-established parties put candidates on the presidential ballot.

The expansion of political freedoms, of course, ultimately requires more than the arbitrary commitments of a powerful executive. If a ruler decides to allow a demonstration "this time," that is not an expansion of political freedom but merely an arbitrary (and likely temporary) enlargement of political space. Hosni Mubarak himself pointed this out when he grumbled about street demonstrators in May 2006, "If they think that what they are doing is an expression of their freedom, they should remember who gave them this chance."[2] Although such openings can be good in themselves, political freedom grows only when the ability of citizens to use political space is codified through a clear policy change: a decree, law, regulation, or judicial ruling. Political freedom is enhanced when one can plan and act with assurance that one's ability to act will not be arbitrarily constrained. Political space can be arbitrary and ephemeral; political freedom is tangible and lasting.

To be secure, political freedom must be enforced as well, and that requires a judiciary that is independent and committed to individual rights and equality under the law. American democracy assistance should continue to go to seminars for Arab judges on judicial independence and the rule of law. But in an environment where judges' hiring and promotion are subject to executive whim and where judges themselves can be prosecuted for failing to bow to executive will, even well-trained judges cannot be expected to act as though they are independent. This is another obvious example of the way American assistance projects, absent supportive diplomatic dialogue, can have little effect. In the case of judicial independence, as in the case of political freedoms overall, the initial step is persuading Arab autocrats to withdraw further—if only marginally—from the political spheres they now dominate.

Where to Pursue Reform?

In the first few years of the Freedom Agenda, the Bush administration tended to favor programs that either targeted states already in crisis, as discussed earlier, or that addressed the entire region, such as those sponsored by the Middle East Partnership Initiative and the Broader Middle East and North Africa Initiative. The rationale for a broad, cross-regional approach was to create demonstration projects in different issue areas and a competitive dynamic between reform-minded Arab leaders, each vying for U.S. recognition and rewards in the form of assistance and trade ties. This approach yielded uneven results, because it relied ultimately on the interest of regional leaders in embracing reform and winning U.S. approval. It did not concentrate resources relative to the importance of the country involved to the regional picture or to U.S. interests. These efforts were also constrained by the limited resources they had to work with. In an environment of regional instability and backlash against reform (and especially against U.S. democracy promotion), a cross-regional approach is likely to yield only small payoffs.

The twenty-one Arab states and the Palestinian territories are situated very differently with respect to political, economic, and social reform. Some Arab leaders have already undertaken fundamental decisions to reform economic structures (Jordan, the United Arab Emirates), education (Qatar), or the distribution of political power (Yemen). Many others remain caught between the risks of reform and the pain of continued stagnation. For a few regimes that were prepared to take limited risks for reform—notably those of the Jordanian and Moroccan monarchs—the recognition and limited benefits the Bush administration put on offer were effective incentives. The competitive dynamic sometimes backfired, however, causing some leaders, as in Syria, to give up momentum in their domestic reforms in order to avoid appearing to bow to regional or American pressure. At times the U.S. government set aside its regionwide approach in favor of places such as the Palestinian territories that were of special interest to the United States. Currently some states in the region, such as Lebanon and Iraq, face such severe governance challenges that further democratic exercises will only fracture society more. In other cases the state is perhaps too strong for its own good.

Some Arab states' fates will weigh more heavily on the region's future than others. Although the small gulf emirates may make swift progress in implementing economic and educational reforms, their small populations and geographical isolation mean that their societies' progress and prospects will have only marginal effects on their larger Arab neighbors. But the future of Egypt, with 70 million people, of Iraq, with 25 million, and of Algeria, with 30 million, will have a decided effect not only on the Middle East's overall developmental health but on the progress of economic globalization. In the same fashion, the failure of even a single major Arab state to overcome its demographic challenge could result in a destabilization of the region. Imagine, for example, the effect of large-scale social instability in

Egypt or Saudi Arabia on American interests in regional security and stable energy production.

Finally, the United States also has more developed, multifaceted, and interdependent relations with some Arab states than with others, and these relations provide leverage even as they increase America's risk in promoting change. Whether and how to link the imperative of reform to other aspects of bilateral relations with key Arab states such as Egypt and Saudi Arabia is a central challenge for the United States in constructing a viable and effective pro-reform strategy. In the coming term the U.S. government should focus its efforts on key Arab states with which it has multifaceted relationships and whose stability and success carry the greatest weight. American efforts should be focused on helping cultivate the political will and leadership in those countries that are necessary to decide upon and implement important structural reforms in politics and economics. In some cases, carefully structured incentives provided by the United States might make a decisive difference in the attitudes of political leaders toward reform.

Egypt and Saudi Arabia stand out for both the depth of their relationships with the United States and the influence their domestic stability and evolution exert on broader regional developments. America's attitude toward its closest Arab allies will greatly determine the credibility and effect of U.S. efforts toward political reform regionwide—and so far the record is not an encouraging one. Morocco, Algeria, and Yemen represent a second tier of Arab states with sizable populations and noticeable abilities to affect regional prospects, with which the United States has sufficiently close ties to help shape developments. Syria has a troubled relationship with the United States, but its role in the Arab-Israeli conflict and in Lebanese politics, and its shared border with Iraq, enhances the importance of U.S.-Syrian interactions and gives America an additional stake in Syria's future as well as additional leverage over its regime. Jordan, Qatar, Bahrain, and Kuwait represent a third tier of states whose economic and demographic weight in the region may be less but whose political leaders may prove influential and whose relationships with the United States may provide additional American leverage. Pro-reform developments in these states might enhance the momentum of change by providing a demonstration effect, although the tangible effects of developments in these states on other Arab countries are likely to be limited.

Lebanon, Iraq, and the Palestinian territories fall into a special category: they are weak states, incapable of effectively implementing democratic reforms in the face of severe internal challenges. Yet these are the countries in which the Bush administration pressed hardest, using diplomatic and financial means, for democratic progress, notably for open elections. As a result, these governments now face more difficult challenges than ever before. Lebanon, Iraq, and the Palestinian Authority deserve concerted, high-level American attention—but that attention should be focused on state-building rather than on democratization.

The recommendation that America focus its efforts first on Arab states with which it has the closest ties brings me back to the thorny question of conflicting priorities. What leverage do American policymakers have to alter the calculus of the Saudi or Egyptian regimes—leverage that they are actually willing to use? Is it possible for the United States to preserve working relationships with regimes whose assistance remains essential across a range of policy areas even while pushing them to give up considerable amounts of power?

I believe the answer is an unequivocal yes, mainly because the assumption that promoting democracy will cost us cooperative relations with Arab regimes is not wholly true. First, the caricature of the relationship between the United States and Arab governments—that of a fruitful partnership carefully crafted by generations of wise diplomats who have cultivated and assuaged wary Arab leaders—presents a false picture of the nature of U.S.-Arab cooperation. The relationship is in fact far less personal and far more strategic than this caricature suggests. It will therefore prove less sensitive than many people imagine to the strains caused by the United States' injecting a new variable into the equation.

U.S.-Arab cooperation over the past sixty years has rested more than anything on strong foundations of mutual interest. The mutuality of those interests has only grown over time as America's role in the region has become larger and more multidimensional and as American global leadership has had increasingly greater effects on the international environment in which Arab leaders must operate. Such relationships can withstand a greater degree of tension than they have generally witnessed—as indeed has been demonstrated repeatedly since September 11, 2001. As one reformist Arab official told me, "the fact that problems come up does not mean that you have to stop the relationship. The relationship exists because you will have problems, and within that relationship you will solve all the problems."[3]

Riyadh and Washington share interests in the strategic defense of the Persian Gulf and stability in the price of oil, and they still would, even if the United States were to push Saudi Arabia harder on political reform. For better or worse the Saudis have no reliable capacity for self-defense against external threats. No gulf state has the naval power to protect oil shipments to global markets; this has been an American monopoly at least since the United States reflagged Kuwaiti tankers during the Iran-Iraq war in the 1980s. The United States wants the intelligence Saudi Arabia can provide regarding the financing and activities of al Qaeda sympathizers in the kingdom, and the Saudi government wants American intelligence and cooperation regarding the activities of sympathizers outside who might target Saudi interests.

This foundation of mutual interests means that in many cases American conflicts of interest between democracy promotion and strategic cooperation are more apparent than real. U.S.-Egyptian cooperation on Arab-Israeli issues, to take one significant example, may indeed have been established on precarious grounds and greased with copious quantities of American aid money, but it is sustained today for solid reasons of state that have endured for decades.

Indeed, Egyptian behavior over the past several years suggests that far from rejecting cooperation with the United States, Egypt's government at times accelerates its cooperation on the Middle East peace process at moments of heightened American pressure for internal reform. Egypt has even gone so far as to pursue Arab-Israeli diplomacy at times when the Bush administration spurned the effort or looked on with interest but only casual concern for Egypt's investment and its potential payoffs. Egypt volunteered to mediate a Palestinian cease-fire in 2004 to facilitate Israel's withdrawal from Gaza and then to adjust the Camp David accords and move its own troops to the border to enable a full Israeli withdrawal from the Philadelphi corridor between Egypt and Gaza. It did so not to win rewards from Washington but to ensure stability on its remote northern border. And it took these steps in 2004 and 2005, two years in which the United States was more outspoken on democracy issues inside Egypt than it had been in the previous ten years together. American pressure on democracy did not halt Egyptian cooperation on the peace process. If anything, Mubarak accelerated and highlighted his peace process–related activities, perhaps as a way of trying to prove his value to an American audience and thereby lessen the external pressure for reform.

So the United States' conflicts of interest that are often assumed may not prove to be problems in reality. I would go farther to argue that in the current circumstances of the Middle East, America has a powerful case to make to Arab rulers that democratic reform both is in their self-interest and is a fundamental prerequisite for continued U.S.-Arab cooperation. American will be required to offer Arab states a great many security commitments to offset the harmful consequences of Iraq's chaos and Iran's ambitions; Arab states should be expected to match this U.S. investment by making the changes necessary to build internal stability.

Inevitably, the achievement of a new, more stable equilibrium in Arab politics—and of a sustainably positive environment for U.S.-Arab relations—will necessitate short-term disruption and change. America's approach to this process should address the sources of instability in the region and help shape the development of the Arab world in ways that will protect the United States' long-term interest in stability while serving its urgent interest in undermining popular Arab sympathy and support for extremist ideologies that promote violence against America and its allies. Thus America's strategy must work to manage a complex process of change while minimizing its associated costs and risks and shaping the change in a direction that suits the United States' long-term and enduring interests. Balancing the long-term goal of democracy promotion against the constantly felt short-term incentives and imperatives of U.S. foreign policy will be an ongoing challenge, but mechanisms can be developed to address it.

Within a framework that prioritizes political freedom and focuses attention on America's most important regional partners, American goals for the coming period should include specific short-term objectives for each of three core policy arenas: economic, educational, and political reform. The idea of identifying such short-term objectives is both to encourage regional governments to start immediately down a path of comprehensive reform and to demonstrate to their populations the United States' seriousness about this reform. In addition, having immediate-term objectives helps to overcome the natural tendency of American policymakers to push democracy promotion down the priority list in favor of other, more tangible objectives.

Even in the short term, expanding political freedom should be central. The United States should assertively begin pressuring its interlocutors to reduce active state interference in citizens' exercise of basic political rights and to create conditions under which new political movements can emerge and grow. In practice this means loosening controls primarily on free expression and free association. Government-to-government assistance should be focused on improving the responsiveness and transparency of basic government services, from finance to family law and criminal justice, in order to reduce the arbitrary exercise of executive or bureaucratic power and to enhance the flow of information to citizens about government policy. American diplomacy and U.S.-funded nongovernmental programs should encourage political dialogue that engages with, challenges, and tests Islamist ideas and political programs against alternatives and against democratic commitments. And the United States should promote democratic governance within the NGO sector to ensure that these organizations are grassroots and depersonalized.

These steps can be supported with pushes for quick changes in education and economics as well. With respect to economic reform, the short-term goals should include absorbing new job-market entrants through vocational training programs and private sector job-creation efforts, providing credit to youth to help them improve their social and economic integration, and improving the transparency and accountability of government spending to reduce resentment-breeding corruption and provide new information about government activities, a powerful tool for indigenous media and watchdog groups. In the arena of social and educational reform, American policy should focus at first on a simple and urgent goal: getting governments to reduce the use of educational material that incites or inculcates prejudice and hatred.

U.S. policymakers must also keep their eyes on long-term objectives in each of these three arenas. Longer-term goals will keep policymakers both in the region and in Washington focused on the ultimate objective of building a more pluralistic and prosperous Arab world. Again, advancing political freedoms lies at the center, with the other two pillars in supporting roles. The long-term goal is to promote legal and constitutional reforms to enshrine and enhance political rights and freedoms. Police, military, and security institutions require reform to enhance professionalism and bring about depoliticization and depersonalization of these authority structures. America must push as well to improve the rules governing freedom in the context of elections—ballot access more than the balloting itself—in order to encourage open, competitive contests within a more diverse political marketplace.

In the economic arena, goals should include the reduction of income inequality, using transparent rulemaking and information-sharing as tools to chip away at the discretionary authority that government officials and bureaucrats wield today to dispense boons to supportive clients. In the educational pillar, the objective should be to reform teacher training and national curricula to emphasize the critical-thinking and problem-solving skills that are essential to a knowledge economy and equally essential to help inoculate young people against the propaganda of the radicals. The United States should also strive to enhance civic education to promote citizen engagement, toleration, and pluralism in popular approaches to politics.

These three arenas for action are clearly interrelated and can be mutually reinforcing, as when vocational education promotes easier absorption of young people into a tight labor market. If a society democratizes its politics without building strong state institutions, its electoral process may be easily steamrolled by populist forces, often antidemocratic ones. This is the historical lesson of Weimar Germany and more recently of elections in Lebanon, Iraq, and the Palestinian territories. Likewise, a society that democratizes without enshrining individual rights in law or building civil society institutions may well produce a passive and demobilized population that is subject to manipulations of the political process at the hands of elite power groups or the regime itself.

Still, these three arenas of reform can undermine one another in certain areas, such as when privatization of state-owned industry, required to attract greater foreign investment and reduce state domination of the economy, throws workers out of well-paid, secure jobs. All good things do not necessarily go together, and U.S. officials should take care in setting priorities to ensure that the changes they advocate in one arena do not undermine more important or more urgent objectives elsewhere.

How to Pursue Reform?

Can the United States change its diplomatic dialogue with Arab states from one in which reform is one among disparate items on a long agenda to one in which reform is part and parcel of U.S.-Arab cooperation? I believe it can, and that the case for reform, properly articulated, should resonate with Arab leaders, who are increasingly nervous over regional trends toward radicalization and over the apparent decline of American power in the Middle East.[4] Arab leaders feel keenly the threats from radical Islam within their own societies, while radical leaders outside their borders claim the mantle of

Islamic and Arab leadership for themselves. The critique local Islamists provide of regime performance at home and abroad echoes the rhetoric trumpeted by Iran and Hizballah. Bitter experience teaches that repressing the region's radicals does not remove the threat they pose; instead, repression in one country often pushes radicals to safer havens from which they can wreak more terrible damage. The appeal of Islamist radicalism lies in its ideology of revolutionary resistance to the stagnation and suffering in many Arab societies today. Countering that ideology requires a positive alternative vision of the future in which moderation, tolerance, and peace provide greater benefits and opportunities than resistance and violence.

Moreover, Arab rulers face a dilemma: they know that regional stability demands their close cooperation with the United States, but it does so at a moment when their publics view America's regional role with fury. Enhancing Arab cooperation with American regional diplomacy, it appears, will thus require enhanced repression at home. To extract Arab rulers from this dilemma, and to be sustainable and effective in countering the region's radical axis, American-Arab cooperation must rest on a new foundation of partnership among the United States, moderate Arab governments, and their mostly moderate citizens—a partnership designed to produce a better future for the people of the Middle East.

Within the context of relationships forged in mutual interests, the United States has major cards to play with its Arab interlocutors. For some, such as the Saudis, the card is the American security umbrella. For others, notably Egypt, money is an important card. Flows of aid and arms from the United States to Arab countries have proved important to cementing strategic cooperation on a host of issues, most notably Arab-Israeli peace. American economic and military assistance can also be used to give autocratic governments incentive to liberalize, but it is likely to be most effective if used as a carrot more than a stick. Similarly, U.S. aid money can be employed to help to ease a political transition and to blunt radicalism in a successor regime.

The question of conditioning U.S. bilateral aid to Arab governments on their commitment to democratic reform is perhaps the most controversial issue in building a pro-reform policy. On the one hand, existing aid programs designed to encourage gradual reform through consensual projects have a limited record of success, suggesting that "tougher" measures are appropriate. On the other hand, altering the composition and conditions of long-standing U.S. aid programs in countries such as Egypt—close allies with real poverty and development needs—is likely to induce a popular backlash, perhaps more quickly than any other American policy shift.

Some analysts simply reject the idea of conditionality as inconsistent with the principle of "partnership" with the Arab world in promoting reform. Conditioning aid on internal changes is, in this view, too coercive and likely counterproductive. If the type of partnership the United States seeks is solely with Arab governments, then that may be true. But if by partnership one means partnering with Arab citizens who want to improve their lives and who individually are the ones who choose to stay at home or to migrate, to remain productive citizens or to join a violent radical movement, then conditioning American relations with and assistance to Arab governments on their behavior toward their citizens seems wholly appropriate. While maintaining working relations with Arab leaders, the United States must never fail to emphasize its alliance with Arab citizens in their struggle for a better future.

Rather than reducing extant amounts of aid or placing new conditions on long-standing aid, the United States should in most cases focus on building political conditionality into all *new* bilateral assistance proposals. In countries where the U.S. government plans to increase development assistance, such as Morocco, it should ensure that new U.S. funds are spent with greater autonomy than in the past, are more directed toward nongovernmental actors, and are more focused on democracy and governance programs.

One lever already available is that several Arab governments are interested in qualifying for development funds from the Millennium Challenge Corporation, created in 2004, eligibility for which includes governance criteria.[5] Yemen's President Ali Saleh was shocked to hear from Secretary of State Rice in November 2005 that his country could not receive Millennium Challenge funds because of its atrocious record on corruption, but the realization prompted him to undertake internal reforms with new energy.[6] Only a few of the poorest Arab countries, however, meet the Millennium Challenge Corporation's maximum income criteria—they are mostly too rich to join.

In countries where a political transition is a realistic possibility (highly unlikely in any Arab country except perhaps Egypt in the near future), carefully structured bilateral packages can provide incentives for desired change to overcome the specific concerns of recalcitrant governments. Egypt, America's largest Arab aid recipient excluding Iraq, agreed in 1998 to a reduction in assistance of 10 percent per year, despite the country's continued need for development aid.[7] The Bush administration debated whether and how to condition a new package of American aid to Egypt but achieved no policy consensus and in the end requested a continuing level of $415 million in economic assistance for fiscal year 2008.[8] This small amount of aid, down from a peak of $815 million in 1998, is unlikely to serve well as leverage for further reforms in Egypt. An alternative approach, given Egypt's continued desire for development aid—both for practical purposes and as a symbol of U.S. commitment—would be to offer a new multiyear package of significant economic aid. A portion of this package would go to direct budget support for the Egyptian government, but certain amounts would be carefully targeted to government sectors that need reform, and a certain amount would be set aside for USAID to spend on democracy assistance independent of Egyptian government oversight. The package would also include annual benchmarks on reforms that would be evaluated jointly and ultimately approved by Congress.

At the same time, the United States can and should use regionwide assistance programs to build new relationships, centered on reform, with Arab government agencies, the private sector, and nongovernmental groups. Regional programs will attract governments that are already committed to pro-reform policies, providing a reward for good policy choices as well as a demonstration effect for other countries in the region. They are unlikely, however, to move governments that are resistant to change.

The most efficient and transparent way to implement this approach would be a new U.S.-Arab Democracy Challenge Account. It would be modeled in part on the Millennium Challenge Corporation, which was also explicitly designed to change the incentive structure for governments in making domestic policies, but it would be more multifaceted in implementation. The Democracy Challenge Account (DCA) would be less focused on low-income countries than the Millennium Challenge Corporation and would thus have less restrictive income criteria for eligibility. The DCA would include government-to-government assistance for countries that met certain governance-related criteria and clearly demonstrated their commitment to implementing a path toward democratization and the rule of law. It would focus money on helping governments implement reforms that would further advance democratic development and provide additional tools to local democracy activists. For example, DCA funds could support the development of transparency mechanisms within government agencies: offices that notify the public of proposed or new government regulations, publicize government contracts, and publish government budgets and expenditure records. DCA money could also go to strengthening the research and public information activities of parliamentary bodies, increasing their capacity to play an effective role while increasing their transparency to the public. Governments' ability to access DCA funds would be conditional on their enabling local civic groups to operate freely and to receive U.S. government democracy assistance themselves. This would create a financial incentive for governments to protect associational freedom and development. It would also allow U.S. officials to match financial support for top-down and bottom-up reform efforts in a given country.

Reform-focused assistance should not neglect the military and security services of Arab countries, but the United States must avoid the temptation to condition its existing military assistance to Arab states on political reform. Military assistance is a tempting target for those who want to impose political conditions on aid, because its dollar value is large and it engages even countries that do not need or want U.S. development aid. By and large, though, America's military assistance programs in the Arab world help to secure high-value cooperation with American strategic goals while preserving local militaries' reliance on U.S. equipment, spare parts, and training and thereby constraining them from overambitious undertakings, including unwarranted interference in domestic politics.

The United States should seek to expand its military training and exchange programs (called IMET). Ongoing cooperation with and training of Arab military officers helps promote the professionalization and independence from politics of Arab military institutions, and this in turn produces a more favorable climate for democratic development in a part of the world where military meddling in business and politics has been long-standing.[9] Given the military's role in upholding autocracy, U.S. dialogue with military and security officers might result in new aid packages targeted to ease their concerns about change: specific assistance to provide job retraining, investment credits, or even pensions to help military officers reduce their economic dependence on autocratic governance structures and transition to civilian life when they leave uniform. Military-to-military dialogue and U.S.-based training and exchange programs can also help build consensus among U.S. and Arab military officers on the role that political and social stagnation plays in radicalizing young people, thereby building the military's constituency for reform and bolstering higher-level U.S.-Arab diplomacy along the lines suggested earlier.

Conditioning military aid might be appropriate in limited circumstances, such as where there is evidence of human rights abuses by recipient agencies, diversions of funds, or direct interference by the military in political affairs. But in general military aid should be an expression of America's commitment to the bilateral relationship and an incentive for Arab governments to maintain military and intelligence cooperation throughout uncertain times.

Despite the failings of the Middle East Partnership Initiative, continuing official U.S. democracy assistance to nongovernmental organizations in the Arab world is important both symbolically and practically. Some argue that the conflict-of-interests problem prevents U.S. officials from designing and implementing forceful or effective democracy assistance projects. I disagree. Independent American sources of democracy assistance, such as the nonpartisan National Endowment for Democracy, play a crucial role and can often undertake projects or support grantees that are too politically sensitive for U.S. government agencies to deal with. But eliminating official U.S. democracy assistance in favor of these nongovernmental efforts would be a mistake. The symbolic importance of devoting official American resources to supporting local democrats is worth preserving, and some local activists may prefer the public profile and possible protection conveyed by official American support to the "under the radar" approach of nongovernmental funding. Moreover, if one supposed advantage of nongovernmental aid is that it can be disavowed by nervous or ambivalent U.S. officials, that can sometimes prove as much a liability as an asset. Officially funded projects give all relevant U.S. officials a stake in their success or failure and can better demand U.S. official attention when they need diplomatic backup.

U.S. democracy assistance, like diplomacy, should be focused on advancing political freedoms and on supporting Arab NGOs that work toward that end. Literacy projects and trade promotion should be funded by USAID and the Commerce Department, respectively—they should not siphon off democracy funds on the argument that reading or microenterprise has some tangential relationship to democratic values or the democratic process. Similarly, short-term exchange programs whose primary value is the building of social bridges between Americans and Arabs are the natural and rightful province of the State Department's Bureau of Public Diplomacy. But just as encouraging Arabs to embrace democratic values will not necessarily lead them to embrace American policies, helping Arabs learn about America will not necessarily lead them to embrace American-style democracy.

The U.S. government should also seek to enhance the role of the American private sector in promoting liberal reform. The Democracy Challenge Account could include incentives (for example, loan or investment guarantees, tax incentives, and favorable credit) for American businesses to expand their relations with Arab counterparts in countries that are committed to meaningful economic *and* political reform. This private sector program might be similar to the incentives provided by the U.S. government to U.S. businesses to invest in Israel and the Palestinian territories in support of the Middle East peace process in the early 1990s.[10]

Hedging against Conflicts of Interest

Beyond manipulating aid money, there are lesser but still concrete steps the United States can take to reduce the likelihood that a more assertive pro-reform policy will undermine U.S.-Arab cooperation on other issues or that successor Arab governments might reverse policies important to the United States. Wherever possible, the United States should work to anchor salient Arab government cooperation with U.S. goals in international commitments—multilateral or to an international governmental organization—rather than simply to the bilateral relationship with this country. In the worst case, should a friendly government fall to radical nationalist or Islamist forces, policies that are most directly tied to a bilateral relationship with the United States are most likely to be targeted for revision, whereas broader international obligations may retain a stronger claim. Instruments to enable this sort of hedge might include multilateral conventions on topics such as terrorist financing and agreements with institutions such as the World Bank on issues like corruption and financial governance; maritime treaties (such as the Law of the Sea Treaty) that provide for freedom of navigation; and a new regional security regime in the Persian Gulf that will address Arab-Iranian tensions there, tie the states of the Gulf Cooperation Council more closely together, improve their ability to contribute to their own defense, and simultaneously codify their reliance on an American security umbrella.

This approach should also inform future U.S. trade policy in the Arab world and any further efforts to use trade as a means to achieve broader economic or political reform. Bilateral free trade agreements proved, under the Bush administration, to be of limited effect in these areas; they are also vulnerable to changes in political regime. By contrast, international and regional trading regimes that include strong rule-of-law mechanisms might better protect business ties from political backlash while supporting more liberal domestic economic policies and commercial law development. American investment and trade may not be a strong enough pull to reverse decades of Arab government economic policy and shake loose the economic underpinnings of Arab authoritarianism, but the demands of the global economy are relentless, and large, multilateral trading regimes help to enforce and incentivize the reforms that the global economy demands.

The United States can also hedge against any backlash in U.S.-Arab strategic cooperation by working with international partners to advance reform in Arab states. The United States and the European Union have divergent concerns about the nature and pace of reform in the Arab world. Europe's concerns about labor migration and its fast-growing Muslim immigrant communities lead the EU to prioritize economic development over other arenas for progress. Still, the United States and its European allies are united on the *goal* of democratic reform as expressed in the Sea Island G8 statement of 2004. The G8 states also made clear at Sea Island their view that Arab civil society and business actors, not merely regional governments, should play a primary role in guiding reform.

European governments and nongovernmental organizations have been active in global democracy promotion for years, and some European democracy assistance groups, such as the German party institutes, have long histories in the Arab world. American and European funders and implementing organizations such as the National Endowment for Democracy and the Westminster Foundation should coordinate regularly—not only at the level of operatives in the field but also at the leadership level. Newer entrants to the field of global democracy promotion, such as Japan, should also be encouraged to coordinate on core issues with Western partners. Most fundamentally, Western governments should unite around the principle that democracy assistance is not an improper or illegitimate intervention in domestic affairs and that local democracy activists' freedom of association is at stake in their ability to reach out for, request, and receive the support of the international community in their work. In other words, access to democracy assistance is an element of Arab activists' basic human rights.

Finally, American policymakers wary of what newly democratic governments in the Arab world might decide about relations with Washington should remember that newly elected governments in newly democratic Arab states will have to face, first and foremost, the pent-up demands of their citizens for improved social, economic, and political welfare. Anti-Americanism may win them some applause on the stump, but isolating their nations from a source of aid and trade, the world's largest market, will not help them balance budgets at home. Expressing anger at Israel might well be worth withdrawing an ambassador from Tel Aviv. But the Egyptian Muslim Brotherhood knows it cannot win a war with Israel, and a new Brotherhood-led government, which might be unable to rely on the loyalty of the Egyptian military, would be unlikely to try.

In sum, the United States has considerable tools with which to temper the perceived conflicts between democracy promotion and other strategic goals. By breaking down the goal of democratic advancement into nearer-term objectives that are closely related to the actual expansion of political freedom and closely tied to the local circumstances of the country in question, American policymakers can break up the ambitious, amorphous, and uncertain task of democratization into realistic tasks and objectives. By looking ahead to anticipate where conflicts of interest are likely to emerge, they can make choices in advance that can either head off conflicts or decisively resolve them in a fashion that reduces or removes the target government's ability to wield strategic cooperation as leverage against U.S. pressure to liberalize.

Perhaps most important, by recognizing where apparent conflicts are not in fact meaningful, Americans can resolve not to allow appearances to guide foreign policy choices in those instances. In many ways, acting according to fears of conflicts of interest and Islamism can create self-fulfilling prophecies, as misguided policies lower the credibility and effect of American efforts and further strengthen the views of Arab governments that America's democracy promotion policy is stronger in word than in deed.

It is critically important that when real conflicts of interest exist, the United States communicate clearly and honestly both its expectations regarding democratic reform and the way it views reform within the scope of its other regional interests. Being transparent in communications with

Arab governments about reform enhances America's effectiveness by giving local reform activists cover for their own efforts. Transparency also helps protect the United States from accusations of hidden agendas or secret deals with dictators. There will inevitably be times and places in which the United States government will make the judgment to downplay its campaign for democratic reform in favor of some high-value, short-term objective or out of concern for possible negative outcomes. In such cases the credibility of any further American advocacy of democracy will hinge on the credibility of America's overall pro-democracy effort. Where the United States' mix of interests dictates a softer approach, officials should acknowledge that openly while holding out the goal of democratic freedom for all. As one U.S. diplomat stationed in the Middle East told me, "That's our job, and what bothers me a little bit about our myth is that making those necessary accommodations and balancing our interests is somehow either duplicitous [or] distasteful."[11]

CHAPTER SEVEN

The Algerian
Nightmare

I N THE YEARS since the Algerian crisis of late 1991, Islamist political
movements have become a regular part of the political scene in every
Arab country, and Islamist ideology presents the main alternative to
pan-Arabism or local nationalisms in every society in the region. The religious discourse of the Islamists is now unavoidably central to Arab politics.
But the "lesson of Algeria"—that Islamists will use democratic elections
solely as a ticket to absolute power and that Western governments will
accept the use of state security forces to block this prospect—has been well
learned in the Arab world.

Obviously, with Islamist movements as widespread, long lasting, and
deeply rooted in society—and as apparently popular—as they have proved
in the years since the Algerian coup, the United States must develop a more
nuanced and effective policy toward the inclusion of Islamist groups in Arab
politics if it is to successfully advance Arab democracy. But to do so American policymakers need to gain a better understanding of the differences
between the many types of Islamist movements and parties now on the
Arab political stage and then to develop a more variegated approach to the
different groups.

The extant discussion of Islamist movements in the scholarly and policy
literature is of little use in this effort. Conventional academic and policy
discussions label Islamists either "moderate" or "radical," generally catego-
rizing them according to one of two rather loose and unhelpful criteria. The

first is violence: radicals are those who are willing to employ violence to achieve their vision of an Islamic society; all those who refrain from violence are "moderate." This begs the question of how to judge groups who do not themselves engage in violence but still condone, justify, or even actively support the violence of others. For example, Sheik Yusuf Qaradawi, a popular Islamist preacher and television personality, abjures violence against Arab regimes, especially that of his host government, Qatar, but continues to support Palestinian terrorism against Israeli targets.[1]

A second, only somewhat more restrictive criterion used by many analysts to distinguish between "radicals" and "moderates" is whether the groups or individuals in question "accept the procedural elements of participating in elections," or, to put it plainly, accept the rules of the democratic game.[2] Popular sovereignty is no small concession for traditional Islamists, many of whom reject democratically elected government as a usurpation of God's sovereignty. Yet commitment to the procedural rules of democratic elections is not the same as commitment to democratic politics or governance. This is most clearly evident in the case of the Algerian Islamic Salvation Front (FIS), which joined elections with a slogan calling for "No laws. No constitution. Only the laws of God and the Koran."[3] Moreover, as numerous philosophers have pointed out, open elections without guarantees of the individual's rights and freedoms quickly devolve into a tyranny of the majority. In a U.S. Institute of Peace report on Islamist politics, Judy Barsalou noted that many observers were willing to accept Islamists' commitment to the rules of electoral democracy "without regard to their vision of what shape a future Islamic state might take."[4]

Crude dichotomies such as moderate versus radical, then, cannot guide U.S. policy in a high-risk endeavor, both because they are too blunt and because they are ultimately unrevealing about aspects of Islamist politics that are of the greatest concern to the United States. Definitional ambiguity serves only to heighten the uncertainty and dangers policymakers face in deciding whether or how to engage with Islamist movements and politicians, and it is unhelpful in understanding the challenges Islamist movements really pose to democratic politics in the Middle East and to U.S. foreign policy. Instead, let me propose a basic, tripartite typology of Islamist movements and suggest the different U.S. approaches that are relevant to each type.

The first and clearest category consists of the relatively small but important group of radical, ideologically driven movements that one can call by the names used for them in the Middle East itself: *jihadist*, for their commitment to violent struggle as the sole means to achieve their goals, and *takfiri*, for their readiness to label other Muslims heretics, apostates, and therefore justifiable targets of violence. Such groups include al Qaeda, of course, along with its affiliates and allies in Iraq, Algeria, and elsewhere in the Muslim world.

Takfiri groups hold a worldview of utter opposition to the United States' role in the Middle East and to the extant system of Arab states. These groups are not interested in formal politics of any variety, save the strict pan-Islamic state they envision setting up once they have toppled the existing governments of their region. They proclaim violent resistance as a religious obligation and as the only appropriate means to revise social and political relations in the corrupt societies in which they live. They reject the current autocrats because of their perceived failure to adhere to Islamic tenets, and they reject democracy as a violation of God's sovereignty over humankind.

The goals of *takfiri* groups are universal and far-reaching—they are not limited to a particular location or a particular political achievement. The scope of these actors' ambitions, their insistence on ideological consistency, and their commitment to revolutionary violence trumps any possible interest such groups might have in political participation within a pluralist framework. For this reason, such groups are highly unlikely to be "moderated" or "tamed" through any conceivable political process. Because they are committed to working outside the system, they are irrelevant to the question of whether Islamist movements can be successfully integrated into a democratic Arab future. They will endanger that future, just as they endanger the present.

The second category includes what one might call "local" or "nationalist" militant Islamist movements. These movements share ideological tropes with the bin-Ladenists, particularly an interpretation of their religion and their political environment that justifies and even requires violence as a means to realize their political goals. But they combine these ideological tenets with a specific political grievance and focus their goals and activities on a specific political arena. Such groups include Hizballah in Lebanon, Hamas and Palestinian Islamic Jihad in the West Bank and Gaza, and the

Islamist militias in Iraq, both Shiite and Sunni in identity. At the most extreme end of this category, very close to the *takfiri* movements, are those such as the Salafist Group for Preaching and Combat (GSPC) in Algeria, at least through 2005.[5]

Two characteristics set this type of Islamist movement apart from both the jihadists and the purely political movements I describe next. First, they combine their Islamist ideology with a specific set of local political demands that are the focus of their activity and the core concern of their supporters. Unlike the bin-Ladenists, they seek and benefit from the vocal support of a given local community. Hizballah's twin concerns are Shiite empowerment within Lebanon and "resistance" against Israel next door. For the Palestinian Islamist movements, the obvious grievance is with Israel: its existence, its military occupation of the West Bank, and its denial of Palestinian national aspirations. The inclusion of specific political grievances in these groups' political agendas and their close links to specific constituencies mean that occasionally they will engage in political bargaining with other groups in society—but their use of violence as a backstop for their legitimacy severely compromises their capacity to be transformed into fully political actors. Several groups in this category have made the leap to formal politics, using a local democratic opening to legitimate and institutionalize their presence in political life. Hizballah was the first, capturing twelve seats in the Lebanese parliament in the elections of 1992, followed by the Shiite militias of Iraq in 2005 and Hamas in 2006.[6]

The second notable common characteristic of the local militant groups is that they all exist in weak or failing states (or nonstates, in the case of Hamas), where the central government has proved incapable of providing basic security for all its citizens or where the state itself is an arena of contention between competing groups in society. The lack of state capacity enables these movements to wield their weapons with a good deal of support from their local communities. The movements' armed activities serve not only to advance the ideological cause but also to protect local constituents from depredation at the hands of the state or communal rivals.

But their armed status inevitably casts a pall over any progress toward democracy in these societies, because it prevents any application of the basic principle of equality under law. The militants can use their armed capability as a sort of extrasystemic veto over democratic political decisions. Moreover, the extra status these groups enjoy because of their militant activity makes them view a shift into pluralist democratic politics as a step down from their current privileged position in society. As Martin Kramer noted, "these movements have a strong sense of entitlement, and a record of rejecting offers of political inclusion that do not privilege them. The cost of bringing these movements in [to the political system] is high . . . because they insist on retaining their mini-state privileges."[7]

Hizballah pioneered this approach, taking the plunge into competitive politics with its weapons in hand in 1992. Other groups in the region have followed.

Formal politics does offer advantages to these groups. First, it provides them a way to bring material benefits to their local constituents. Political participation is also a way for these movements to institutionalize and insulate their role in society, even should their use of arms become less welcome or less legitimate. Formal politics helps them hedge their bets. They can use the political process to protect their armed status by blocking developments such as peace agreements with Israel or power-sharing agreements with Iraq's Sunni communities that would weaken the rationale for their holding firepower. That groups like these choose to run in elections is itself evidence of the extent to which electoral legitimacy is becoming a norm among Arab citizens. To some extent Hamas chose to run in the Palestinian legislative elections because its supporters expected it to and wanted to be able to vote for Hamas against the rival Palestinian faction Fatah in a process of open political competition.

Thus, although these movements may participate in formal politics, they do not view political processes and institutions as authoritative. In many cases they have demonstrated their readiness to use arms to trump or veto political decisions with which they disagree. In Hamas's case, weapons acquired for "resistance" against Israel were occasionally turned against Fatah, a secular nationalist party that also wields arms against domestic opponents. Ultimately, when political negotiations between Fatah and Hamas broke down, Hamas used its violent capability to take over the territory of the Gaza Strip from the Fatah-dominated Palestinian Authority. Hizballah's leaders, for their part, claim never to have used their weapons against other Lebanese communities, but only against Israel. Yet the movement's violent capabilities still hang as a sword of Damocles over the Lebanese polity, which is acutely sensitive to the possibility of renewed civil conflict. In addition, Hizballah's military actions against Israel have an indirect influence on internal Lebanese debates, because cross-border attacks by Hizballah are likely to provoke Israeli retaliation, which can damage Lebanese civilian communities and national infrastructure.

The fundamental challenge that groups such as Hamas and Hizballah pose to U.S. foreign policy and to Arab democratization is their use of violence, not their Islamist character or ideology, although the latter is used to justify the former. Such movements could not have emerged into this dual role of militant political party in a strong state like Egypt; indeed, whenever the Muslim Brotherhood or its offshoots in Egypt developed violent capabilities, the government crushed it mercilessly. Only regimes with insufficient capacity to enforce their monopoly on violence and with weakened legitimacy for their governance and political institutions are compelled to allow such compromised groups to participate in politics with their weapons in hand. As long as states such as Lebanon remain too weak to contain or reverse the armed activity of militants like Hizballah, there is little hope of full democracy or meaningful equality under law.

In weak states riven by social conflict and surrounded or permeated by daily violence, democratic elections rarely produce outcomes that contribute to stability, regardless of their geographic, religious, or cultural context. Seen from this perspective, the challenge groups such as Hizballah and Hamas pose to democratic politics in the Arab world takes shape as one that is not unique to the Middle East or even the Islamic world. It is a challenge seen in weak or failed states worldwide. In divided societies and in the absence of stable governmental institutions, democratic elections tend to exacerbate social divisions and increase the likelihood of conflict.[8]

Clearly, in such cases elections are not the best mechanism for promoting or enforcing democratic norms and procedures. Those concerned to advance both democratization overall and the peaceful integration of Islamist movements within democratizing systems must first work to resolve conflict, strengthen political institutions, and bolster the basic governing capacity of the state. When state police, prosecutors, and judges are able to protect citizens' security and property, and when government is capable of providing basic services beyond security, such as food and housing, then the justification of armed factions for retaining their arms is severely degraded.

Just as clearly, the standard menu of U.S. democracy promotion programs is totally inappropriate to the circumstances of the weak states in which these militant movements reside. Most democracy promotion efforts focus on weakening executive power by building up alternative power centers: civil society organizations that mobilize citizens to press their demands on the state, legislative bodies to oversee and check executive performance, free media to expose flaws in governance. But in Lebanon, Gaza, and Iraq, the executive authority of the state is already overwhelmed by challenges and requires strengthening.[9] Instead of elections, institution-building and conflict resolution should be key foci for external intervention in cases like Iraq, Lebanon, and Palestine, as they are key prerequisites for a meaningful and stable transition to democracy in these societies.[10]

Thinking of Hamas and Hizballah primarily as Islamist groups rather than as nationalist militants obscures the search for solutions to the problems these groups pose for democratic politics. Recognizing the role of social conflict and state weakness in facilitating the rise and consolidating the presence of armed Islamist movements ought also to clarify the stakes for the more capable Arab states of carrying out successful reforms in order to preserve stability and state capacity. States facing the most significant challenges to their long-term governability or the direst indicators of potential social instability are places where new social contracts must be most quickly introduced and most soundly developed in order to stave off the sort of state erosion or state failure that would enable violent Islamists to stake a claim to public loyalties. Algeria, for example, only recently and partially emerged from a long period of civil conflict, ought to continue on its path to political liberalization and integration of peaceful Islamist movements into freer and more open politics. If it does not, and if the country does not likewise address enduring socioeconomic challenges through economic reform, integration of indigenous communities, and sound resource management, then the state may lose ground to the lingering militants, who claim to represent the interests of the downtrodden and dispossessed. Algeria's secular military government managed to sustain the support of most Algerians throughout a decade-long civil conflict with militant Islamists. But if it does not make political and economic openness a meaningful reality—for peaceful supporters of Islamist parties, for Berbers, and for others—then it risks losing that public loyalty and its ability to control the direction of Algeria's political evolution. The Algerian government cannot fight the arguments of the *takfiri* groups merely by invoking the public's fear of chaos—it must put a positive alternative on offer.

Finally, it should be clear from the preceding analysis that the results of the elections in Iraq, Lebanon, and Palestine in 2005 and 2006, in which militant Islamist movements made strong showings and in Palestine won outright, should not be viewed as a foreshadowing of what more open elections are likely to bring in the rest of the Arab world. Hamas won in Palestinian legislative elections first and foremost because of the failure of the Fatah movement and the mainstream Palestine Liberation Organization (PLO) to move Palestinians from occupation to independent governance. This failure was reflected in a variety of spheres, from Yasir Arafat's reckless abandonment of diplomacy and embracing of violence in the fall of 2000 to the endemic corruption and ineffectiveness of the Fatah-led Palestinian Authority. In the context of Israeli reoccupation of large sections of the territories, daily incursions by Israeli forces into Palestinian cities, and no prospect for renewed peace negotiations, Palestinians had little reason to put their faith yet again in the failed Fatah Party. Similarly, in an atmosphere of escalating sectarian violence, Iraqis were rational to give their political support to those who appeared to have the best capacity to protect them from rival communities. In the chaotic wake of the Hariri assassination in Lebanon, with Lebanon's political balance of power up for grabs, Lebanese Shiites were reasonable in giving their votes once again to the movement that had demonstrated its capacity to protect their interests within Lebanon's delicate multiethnic framework. In the context of ongoing conflict, citizens tend to look to communal groups with the capacity to protect them. The electoral successes of the militant Islamists in these three states are no different in this regard from the electoral victories of militants in other weak, conflict-ridden states.

Little of the Arab world, however, is composed of weak states that host armed, nonstate movements. Most of the Arab world's states are strong (too strong, some might say) in the sense of having a monopoly over the means of violence, control over sovereign territory, and effective governing institutions. In the strong states of the Middle East, the Islamists who are active in politics are of a rather different variety from Hamas and Hizballah and present different questions and challenges. Let me now take a closer look at these movements and what they mean for Arab democracy.

This third and largest category of Islamist movements—the category most relevant to discussions of democratic change in the Arab world—comprises groups that eschew violence (at least in their local context) and aspire to participate in the politics of the state within which they live, without any overtly revolutionary goals. Such groups may operate as legal political groupings, like the Islamic Action Front in Jordan and the Justice and Development Party in Morocco, or they may be excluded from "formal" political recognition but still engage in the political process, like the Muslim Brotherhood of Egypt and the Islamist "societies" of Kuwait.

The most prominent group in this third category is the Muslim Brotherhood of Egypt. Although there are legitimate and serious questions to be asked about the Brotherhood's commitment to democracy and the rule of law, it is clear that this movement is not in the same league as al Qaeda (indeed, al Qaeda includes a splinter group that abandoned the Brotherhood and left Egypt years ago). Neither is the Brotherhood really the same as Hamas, another of its descendants, which regularly uses violence against its enemies both foreign and domestic. Rather, leaving aside for a moment its true intentions or motivations, one can say empirically that the Muslim Brotherhood is one of a third category of Islamist groups in the Arab world that reject violence as a means to achieve their political ends and seek to participate in formal political competition according to rules laid down by the regimes under which they live.[11]

Notably, most of these apparently peaceful Islamist movements exist in strong states, often ones in which state forces successfully put down more violent or revolutionary Islamist movements in previous eras. In exchange for greater freedom of action in the social and sometimes the political sphere, Islamists who are still breathing in the wake of these repressive episodes have been willing to recognize the sovereignty and basic legitimacy of the regime. When the choice is between marginalization, existence as an illegal underground, or a legal existence constrained by the state, these groups have chosen to maintain their ability to speak to the broader public by accepting the basic rules laid down by the state. They maintain the goal of transforming society and government into a more "Islamic" model but aim to do so "from below"—that is, by persuading citizens to adopt Islamist ideas and more observant Islamic practices and to demand more Islamist policies from their governments.[12]

The question is whether this initial pragmatic decision to accept the rules of formal politics reflects a broader and more enduring pragmatism or whether these nonviolent movements are simply radical ideologues biding their time. Can this third category of "inside-the-system" Islamists play a constructive role in democratic Arab societies in years to come? And even if so, can the United States accept and live with the ideas and policies they uphold and would likely try to implement once in office?

In attempting to answer these questions, one immediately arrives at a vexing problem: how to assess these movements' claims of political moderation with regard to the principles and practice of liberal democratic politics—and ultimately with regard to policy questions salient to America, such as coexistence with Israel. What does political moderation mean for these groups, and how do we know whether they are indeed moderating?

Even on the relatively fundamental issue of nonviolence, a thorough assessment is difficult. The track record in public politics for these Islamist political movements is in many cases short, and many of the groups that fall into this category today have in the past either engaged in, justified, or associated with people who conducted violence against the state.[13] Some may abjure violence locally but celebrate violent actions against Americans in Iraq or against Israelis. Others may reject violent actions but still label those who carry them out "martyrs."[14] So some caution is in order in assessing what apparent "moderation" means, and any effort to assess a given movement's democratic commitments must rely first and foremost on improved clarity and specificity on the part of the groups themselves in laying out their core beliefs and justifying their stances and behavior.[15]

An Islamist group's attitude toward violence is a necessary but insufficient indicator of its likely ability to play a constructive role in a democratic political system. One might also usefully examine several other aspects of a movement's political views and behavior—three, in particular.[16] First is the movement's attitude toward minorities—especially non-Muslim minorities—and women. Despite the common perception of the Arab world as socially homogenous, in fact the region hosts a wide array of ethnic, sectarian, and religious minority groups with long histories in their locales. Christianity and Judaism have been present in the Middle East longer than Islam itself. Harsh geography and local tolerance have served to protect the health and viability of communities such as the Berbers of North Africa, the Maronites of Lebanon, and the Samaritans of Nablus. Other groups, including Armenians and Circassians, actually relocated to the Arab world to find a haven from persecution at home. Equality under the law for minorities, for women, and indeed for every individual regardless of his or her beliefs or ethnic origin is a basic tenet of human rights norms, yet traditional views of Islamic jurisprudence do not embrace this notion. Confronting and resolving this apparent contradiction and distinguishing between the Islamic community's view of non-Muslims and the state's view of non-Muslim citizens are major tasks for Islamist movements seeking to persuade citizens in a diverse nation of the sincerity of their democratic credentials.

A second focus of attention in determining a movement's relative moderation is its attitude toward political pluralism. No democratic system can thrive in the absence of political pluralism, and unless political parties within that system subscribe to the principles of pluralism, democratic politics can quickly devolve into violence. Questions relevant to pluralistic values include: Does the movement's view of politics allow for a system in which they are one among different tendencies? How willing is a given group to yield power in the event of electoral defeat? How willing are party leaders to forge political coalitions with non-Islamist movements on behalf of common goals? How willing are they to continue their participation in a system that does not regularly reward them with political power? These questions are relevant not only to what an Islamist movement might do if elected to majority status or to high office but also to the question of how thoroughly it embraces basic elements of democratic politics such as alternation of power, pragmatism, and political compromise.

A third important attitudinal question especially relevant to Islamist movements is whether they believe that religious authority should have any sort of veto or constraint on the exercise of the democratic process. The Egyptian Muslim Brotherhood, for example, has now had members in parliament for more than two decades and has developed a reputation for good constituent service, active use of the parliamentary process to challenge the regime and press forward social legislation, and lack of corruption. The movement's leadership invested a great deal of energy, especially in the period after 2004, to giving press interviews clarifying the sincerity of its commitment to democratic politics. Unlike other brotherhood-based movements such as the Jordanian Islamic Action Front, the Egyptian brotherhood has refrained from boycotting even rigged elections. Yet in 2007 the Muslim Brotherhood shocked many in Egypt and abroad by releasing a draft political platform that called for a higher council of religious scholars to evaluate government decisions according to Islamic law. Although the Brotherhood claims this body would be advisory only and would merely realize the Egyptian constitution's claim that Islamic law is the major source of legislation, the intent to develop a religious body as a formal political institution alongside president and parliament raised hackles in many quarters and led several Brotherhood figures to disavow the platform document entirely in an effort to preserve their democratic credentials.[17] Although the platform document was a setback in the Muslim Brotherhood's campaign to be accepted as a benign political actor, it was a revealing document, and the Brotherhood's desire to clarify its views by drafting and releasing such a document itself represents a form of progress in the evolution of Islamist politics in Egypt.

These three attitudes—toward women and minorities, toward political pluralism, and toward Islamic law—can provide some guidance regarding the content of "moderation" for Islamist (and other) political movements and thus some measure of their likely functioning in a democratic political system. But the question remains, how can one assess a group's moderation along these vectors? How does one recognize moderation when one sees it?

The rhetoric espoused by these groups is not an especially useful guide, because many of them insist on their commitment to democracy while making statements or engaging in actions that contradict basic democratic principles such as equality under the law. Indeed, many peaceful Islamist groups appear to thrive on ambiguity regarding their political programs and policy commitments. But if rhetoric is a poor guide, if language is often vague and behavior often contradictory, then how does one know whether apparent moderation is meaningful?

One leading thinker on this question, Jillian Schwedler, argues that moderation that is meaningful in democratic terms will be evident not merely in altered rhetorical commitments but in a party's internal debates. "If an Islamist party struggles with how—indeed, whether—it can justify particular dimensions of democratic participation, in terms of its broader ideological commitments, we can confidently say that it has evolved ideologically when internal policy commitments have shifted toward more inclusivity and tolerance of alternative views." She asserts that "we can identify change in policies that might fairly be considered ideological moderation if we look to internal party debates and documents rather than relying on public statements alone."[18]

But evidence of internal debate is difficult to come by. The major Islamist movements today are only rarely in a position in which they feel the need to undertake such internal debates. In most countries where they are active, they are overwhelmingly dominant among the political opposition and often are the only religiously informed opposition, so they are seldom challenged on the specifics of their religious platforms or on their commitments to pluralism. The relevant questions tend to be asked most frequently by Western journalists or researchers rather than by locals. Yet despite their dominance of the opposition ground, these movements have little prospect of wielding significant governmental authority even if they do win parliamentary elections. Because of the strength of the executive branch of government in these semiauthoritarian regimes, parliamentary control yields little political authority. Thus Islamist movements in the strong states of the Arab world are in a situation that grants them great prominence, even deference, but little practical accountability.

For this reason, two further elements of the political context must be examined to determine the relative moderation of an Islamist movement: the internal transparency of the movement and the degree of overall political freedom in the society in which it operates. Few Islamist political movements enjoy internal democracy—indeed, they tend to have strongly hierarchical internal structures that are opaque to external scrutiny. Internal transparency, by contrast, allows journalists, scholars, and ordinary citizens access to information about a movement's internal debates and struggles, enabling an evaluation like that favored by Schwedler but also providing the movement's constituents access points by which to influence the movement's direction. Internal democracy, in this sense, is an excellent guide to a party's ability to participate in external democracy.

The Moroccan Party of Justice and Development (PJD) presents an interesting case study in this regard. In a highly variegated, multiparty system, and facing competition from an outlawed but still strong Islamist movement that rejects formal politics and calls for an end to the monarchy, the PJD differentiated itself through open and democratic internal governance. The party's internal debates over whether to run candidates in all parliamentary districts in the 2007 elections and whether to attempt to join the government if it did well in the balloting were both quite open to public view. Party activists with different visions for the party competed for leadership positions in internal party elections, and the more pragmatic activists carried the day.

Second, political freedom is a crucial ingredient in the ultimate ability of either citizens, wary regimes, or external observers to accurately evaluate the moderation of Islamist groups. When they are under little pressure to elucidate their views on crucial issues, Islamists enjoy the position of being a sort of empty vessel for the hopes and fears of all those who are dissatisfied with their current political leadership. Polling data demonstrate that supporters of Islamist movements in Morocco and Lebanon come from both secular and religious backgrounds and political preferences; their most notable characteristic is their sense of dissatisfaction with their political status quo.[19] One member of a royal family from the gulf told me, "The only institution expressing freedom in the Arab world today is the mosque. That's why they're popular."[20]

Islamists benefit from being a relatively untested quantity in Arab politics, at least in comparison with the monarchists, socialists, Baathists, Nasserists, and others who have dominated the political stage in the postcolonial Arab world. Voting for an Islamist party or candidate is the clearest way available today for an Arab to cast a protest vote. That Islamists continue to bear the brunt of regime repression, and that their views and platforms remain unchallenged by any other viable movement, only solidifies their reputation as the most authentic opposition.

Islamists benefit organizationally as well as ideologically from the failure of Arab regimes to open political space to new alternatives. Because state repression can never fully shut down discussions and meetings held in the religious context of a mosque or school, Islamists continue to enjoy space to organize, advertise, and mobilize supporters that is denied to secular political activists. Through continued denial of basic political freedoms, Arab regimes in effect protect Islamists from competition by other political opposition movements. By preserving the Islamists as a broad-based, popular, and underspecified political opposition, they also maintain the sense of threat the Islamists present to the interests of secularist and minority groups inside the country and to Western interests outside it.

Thus the current environment in most Arab states—one of tightly controlled politics—is not one that is conducive to helping either local citizens or outside observers assess Islamists' true intentions and goals and thus their compatibility with a democratic system. Indeed, the current environment makes it less likely, rather than more so, that Islamists will be compelled to behave in a way that will make their political attitudes and behavior more moderate or pragmatic or will reveal any more moderate or pragmatic attitudes that might exist among their memberships.

In the final analysis, an Islamist movement's commitment to the democratic process cannot be tested until there is a meaningful political process in which it can choose to engage. A movement's vision cannot be properly understood until public debate forces the movement's politicians to spell out policies beyond the slogan "Islam is the solution." This suggests that the first step necessary to facilitate the proper evaluation of Islamist movements is the expansion of public debate and discussion of political issues and the easing of restrictions on political association and the formation of political parties. Not coincidentally, these steps would also improve the overall quality of political life in Arab states and enhance the long-term prospects for democratic change.

Perhaps also not coincidentally, these steps are precisely those most fiercely resisted by the stronger autocrats of the region, such as Hosni Mubarak. American pressure in favor of these basic political freedoms of speech and association can be made more palatable to leaders like Mubarak if they are put in a context that recognizes security concerns yet draws a clear distinction between probably harmless but untested Islamist movements and those that might present a real threat. If an Arab government is taking meaningful steps to facilitate associational life and cultivate broader debate, and if some movements take advantage of that greater openness to advance violence or other antidemocratic means of influencing politics, then the United States should be willing to tolerate the regime's repression of those forces. But America should not accede to regimes that would use the excuse of radical Islamist activity to crack down on all Islamist groups.

Over time, a legitimate and meaningful political process will present ideological movements with repeated choices that will test their capacity for moderation and compromise in exchange for tangible gains, separating more clearly those who can and cannot play a constructive role in a pluralist system. Politically radical, even violent Islamist elements may remain a factor in many Arab states, but meaningful liberalization of politics will assist in the marginalization of those remaining groups. In Jordan the legalization of political parties in 1992 led to the establishment of at least five different Islamist parties alongside the Muslim-Brotherhood-led Islamic Action Front (IAF). Changes in electoral law and challenges from these other groups on ideology and Palestinian issues spurred fierce debates within the Brotherhood, and some of the more ideological members left the movement. The continued choice between participation as a loyal opposition in parliament and more radical antiregime action also clarified the gaps between the IAF and the violent Islamist fringe, which is tightly watched and repressed by the monarchy's efficient security services.

If, however, the governments of the region that currently host peaceful and participatory Islamist movements fail to make progress toward a meaningful devolution of power in fear (real or feigned) of an Islamist takeover, the results could, paradoxically, strengthen radical Islamist forces. The primary motive for public support of Islamism is fundamental discontent with the political status quo. If a parliamentary system in which nonviolent Islamists participate is perceived as window dressing on autocracy rather than a real opportunity to influence governance, then those discontented with the political stasis will go elsewhere. In such circumstances it is the nonviolent, participatory Islamists who will be discredited while the radicals will grow in popularity. Cultivating Islamist movements that embrace democratic participation and democratic pluralism will be an important part of successful democratization in many Arab societies—but the legitimacy of a moderate Islamist political discourse will hinge on the legitimacy of the democratization process overall.

Whether or not these groups' commitment to democratic pluralism is sincere and irreversible, and whether or not the governments under which they live ultimately deal with them wisely or foolishly, the presence of Islamists on the Arab political stage is indisputable and irreversible. The United States, in crafting democracy promotion strategies for the Arab world, must take good account of them and the roles they play.

The United States need not embrace a one-size-fits-all approach to Islamist movements. Yet some foundations on which to base a nuanced policy must be clarified. The first—and perhaps the hardest for some American experts and policymakers to accept—is that the United States cannot determine which Islamist or other parties are allowed to participate in Arab political competition. Although the United States repeatedly enunciated the principle that political parties with armed militias should not be allowed to participate in Palestinian or Lebanese elections, it could not enforce that principle in either case.[21]

But although the American government cannot determine who gets to play in the game of Arab politics, it can shape the conditions under which regimes decide when and how to open competitive politics and under which political oppositions decide whether or not to participate. The United States must take care to articulate clearly its view of what a truly democratic political process entails and to articulate its concern for a fair process. A fair process entails guarantees of freedom to organize and campaign, not merely the absence of fraud on election day itself. Freedom to organize new parties, for example, and open ballot access ought to be American priorities because they will enable competitors to emerge who can erode the Islamists' status as the embodiment of citizen dissatisfaction with the status quo, challenge their status as the sole viable opposition, and rebut their views on key issues. Once again, basic political freedoms come to the fore as the best focal point for American diplomacy that will advance democratic politics while preserving American interests.

Even if a democratic process has fair rules applied fairly, the United States may still have preferences about which actors it would like to see emerge victorious. Although the United States should be careful to stress concern for process over concern for outcome, that does not mean that it should *not* express concern over outcomes. Pretending to be neutral in the face of a prospective victory by, for example, an anti-Israel Palestinian party or an anti-American Egyptian party fools no one, whereas being honest about American policy preferences and about whose views cause concern is part of a broader effort to conduct more honest and effective public diplomacy in the region. Concern for process over outcome also means not sparing favored parties from criticism if they engage in unfair practices or articulate undemocratic ideas. This is especially important if the favored option in a given case is the ruling party of the existing regime.

In addition to balancing concern for fair processes and progressive outcomes, the United States can set its own criteria for which political parties and movements it will associate itself with, and at what level. The degree of legitimacy, recognition, and interaction bestowed by the U.S. government can reflect the degree of security America feels in the substantive, ideological, and behavioral moderation these groups demonstrate and in the likelihood that their presence in Arab politics will produce positive payoffs for regional democratization as well as for other American interests. America's attitude toward Islamist opposition movements—and indeed, toward any opposition movements—should therefore be varied according to the movements' characteristics and according to the policies of the regime under which they operate. In practice American officials and NGOs already implement this sort of sliding scale, but without clear criteria to determine where a given relationship ought to fall. As a result, the choices made are vulnerable both to errors in judgment and to second-guessing by domestic American voices that might judge on appearances more than on substance and distort what should be a close connection between decisions on engagement and the balance of American interests. A clear framework for engagement will make dealings with Islamist movements more defensible, not only to domestic audiences but also to Arab regimes. With a framework in hand, the United States could disagree with the Mubarak regime over the legitimacy of talking to the Muslim Brotherhood on the basis of principle rather than on the basis of respecting or violating Mubarak's political preferences. Ideally, the guidelines for engagement will provide greater precision and clarity of purpose than exist in policy today. This in turn ought to help correct the misimpressions widespread in the region regarding America's resolute hostility to all Islamist political movements.

The United States should seek dialogue with peaceful Islamist groups where possible, to hedge against the possibility that Islamist parties might in fact triumph in a competitive political process in some Arab countries. The American government should be willing to engage in dialogue with all groups that disavow violence, even if their commitment to democratic principles is not entirely clear—dialogue can elucidate that question. Dialogue does not imply irrevocable recognition, a fact that was demonstrated by the United States' dialogues with the PLO in 1989 and the Taliban (over the disposition of Osama bin Laden) ten years later.[22] In opening such dialogues, future administrations can build on the Bush administration's experience working with Islamist movements in Iraq to generate lessons and guidelines for engagement elsewhere.

Movements that have demonstrated a commitment to pluralist principles—including not just democratic elections but minority protections, individual rights, and equality under law—ought to be candidates for inclusion in American democracy assistance programs and projects. These might include things such as party-building workshops and campaign seminars organized by the American party institutes, the National Democratic Institute and the International Republican Institute. Indeed, some Islamist parties, including Yemen's Islah and Morocco's Justice and Development Party, already fall into this category and participate in these programs.

But the pluralist credentials of these movements—though suggested by their behavior—have yet to be fully tested in practice. Part of implementing a move away from the harmful embrace of elections as the primary symbol of successful democratization is renewing emphasis on other elements of democratic practice that make the system stable and sustainable, especially protections of individual rights and equality. A willingness by Islamist movements to recognize that spiritual authority does not necessarily inhere in the institutions of the state in a way that allows for government enforcement of religious standards is a crucial element in ensuring that a democratically elected Islamist government cannot impose a tyranny of the majority. No Arab state is without ethnic, religious, and other types of minorities whose rights must be protected, and it is democracy's brilliant innovation that it protects those rights in an individual rather than a collective manner, enabling even members of the majority group to dissociate themselves from the beliefs and practices of the majority without fearing the consequences.

If any Islamist movements meet the basic criteria of commitment to nonviolence, to democratic processes, and to pluralist ideals, then ongoing dialogue and interaction with the United States government will enable a better understanding of such movements' policy preferences on issues of concern to the United States, the foundation of those views, and their amenability to influence from an American perspective. On the basis of such understandings, which can be attained only through dialogue and a shared commitment to basic principles, it is possible to imagine a closer and more cooperative relationship than any that currently exists between the United States and any Islamist party in the Middle East or indeed the world.

Moreover, if U.S. officials become convinced through dialogue and observation that some of the Islamist parties now active in Arab politics are truly committed to pluralist values, democratic practice, and policy views not entirely incompatible with American interests, then American policy can treat those movements as true vanguards of democracy with which America will stand against unreasonable decisions and actions by autocratic governments. If, just once, the U.S. State Department spokesperson decried from the podium the harassment of an Islamist opposition leader, it would help to erase the myth that America will not tolerate Islamist success in Arab politics and erase the legacy of Algeria for America's tarnished credibility on democracy among Arab audiences.

Would more open politics in the Arab world really result in Islamist victories? It is certainly true in nearly all Arab states today that the largest political opposition is Islamist in character. However, the Islamist advantage evident in many Arab societies today exists at least in part because of the state's long-standing intolerance of social organizations outside the framework of religion and, in some cases, because of the Islamicization of public discourse encouraged by the state in its attempts to co-opt religious elites. Moreover, the region's experience with Islamist parties has moved beyond the experience of Algeria in 1991, and few Islamist parties today can sustain either the mystique or the simplistic sloganeering that swept the FIS to victory. Even the FIS and Hamas did not win a majority of the popular vote. As a result, it is unclear in many cases whether a more open political process (especially one gradually introduced) would necessarily bring with it commanding majorities for Islamist forces or whether a more diverse marketplace of ideas and meaningful contestation would reduce the grassroots popularity of Islamist movements to manageable levels.

For purposes of cultivating opposition movements alternative to radical Islamists and thus minimizing the risks that Islamists will take advantage of political openings to the detriment of U.S. interests, the most important reforms the United States can push for are those that will strengthen both liberal political movements and the ability of Arab societies to debate, test, and, it is hoped, reject the claims of radical Islamist movements. The United States must press Arab leaders to level the playing field, which is currently tilted against liberal Arab voices. These reforms, not coincidentally, are also the ones most likely to be resisted by governments as undermining their authority: legalizing alternative political parties, establishing or expanding the freedom of associational life, cultivating a freer broadcast and print media, and increasing the diversity of content in national broadcast media. The United States can subsidize the propagation of alternative voices by supporting liberal groups, supporting independent media efforts, and funding the translation and dissemination of key works of Western liberal political philosophy in Arabic.

The United States can also work in its communications with opposition groups and in its training activities for political activists to encourage dialogue between Islamist and non-Islamist pro-democracy opposition movements. To the extent that such groups can agree on goals or rules for a transition to democracy, they can present a powerful set of demands to the existing leadership.

Expanding political freedoms is the best way to level the playing field in Arab politics, which is currently tilted heavily in the Islamists' favor. In a freer environment it will be easier to distinguish among violent Islamists, conservative Islamists, liberal Islamists, Muslim liberals, and secular politicians of all stripes. When all these groups are able to organize, articulate their views, and compete for citizens' loyalty, then it will be clearer both how popular they are and how much of what they say about democracy and nonviolence they really believe.

CHAPTER EIGHT

Conclusion

D EMOCRATIC REFORM IN the Arab Middle East is neither a luxury nor a pipe dream. It is a necessity. Those who view developments in Arab politics during the Bush administration as proof that the Freedom Agenda was both naïve and arrogant now clamor for a "return to realism."[1] But a desire to return to the status quo ante is not realism; it is fatalism. Those who advocate such a return would consign the Middle East to a dark future that will produce unhappy outcomes for Arabs and Americans alike.

Democracy promotion in the Arab world is not an easy path to tread. To succeed at it, the U.S. government must first set to rest its own demons, legacies of the Iranian Revolution and the Algerian civil war. It must overcome its ambivalence about what democracy will mean for this region and for U.S. interests and work instead to prepare—to make choices about what price the United States is willing to pay in order to achieve democratic gains by allied governments; to take steps to reduce the likelihood of undesirable events; and to protect American interests by hedging its bets regarding the outcomes of democratic reform. Only when the various elements of the American government reach consensus on the value of democratic progress and on the prospects for progress in any given country will the U.S. government as a whole be able to send clear messages to Arab autocrats about what the United States expects and what it is willing to do to make that happen.

To develop internal consensus requires mobilizing a dialogue among U.S. government agencies that have stakes in the Middle East but that until now have generally avoided a robust discussion of their different views of the national interest with respect to democratic reform. Not only the Departments of State and Defense must be engaged but also the Commerce Department, the Justice Department (with its law enforcement training programs as well as its counterterrorism work), the Treasury Department, the CIA, and the Energy Department. The interagency process must examine key countries such as Egypt and Saudi Arabia, evaluate the opportunities for democratic progress, and determine how to maximize American leverage while hedging against risk. Convening and leading such an interagency debate and ensuring implementation of its decisions will require energetic leadership from the National Security Council, which until now has largely waited for disputes to filter up for decision, rather than driving the interagency process forward to a conclusion.

The programs put in place by the Bush administration to try to advance Arab democracy were akin to putting a Band-Aid over a gaping wound. The Middle East Partnership Initiative, the Middle East Free Trade Area, and the Broader Middle East and North Africa Initiative were each in their own ways woefully insufficient to the tasks they were set, and all were wasted efforts in the absence of concerted, consistent, high-level support from senior U.S. officials in their diplomacy with Arab leaders. Until American democracy assistance programs engage the most powerful tools the United States can bring to bear—namely, its diplomatic and economic relations with Arab governments—all the small-bore programs in the world will not do the job.

And those tools must be brought to bear not just on behalf of reform writ large but specifically on behalf of expanding political freedom for Arab citizens. Expanded freedom of speech, press, and association is what will enable indigenous groups to raise their own demands for change and allow America to echo and support them, avoiding charges of imperialist imposition. Expanded freedoms will allow new civil society groups to form and nascent ones to grow in an environment in which they can plan their own projects without fear of government interference and make good use of American and other donated funds to support their activities. Expanded freedoms will enable Arab citizens to name and shame leaders who do not live up to their promises as well as political movements—Islamists among them—who rhetorically embrace democracy but fail to practice it. Expanded freedoms will allow new political parties to emerge, present their ideas to citizens, and compete with ruling parties and Islamists. And expanded freedoms will keep all these parties more honest.

As George W. Bush finishes his final term in office, his most prominent foreign policy initiative, the Freedom Agenda, is at risk. It is at risk because the project has been mishandled by bureaucrats afflicted with ambivalence about its goals and means. It is at risk because its failures have gutted its credibility, leaving Arab autocrats to wait out the end of Bush's presidency in the hope of a softer deal from the next president. It is at risk, too, because Bush himself oversold the project to the American public, first by linking it to the faltering bandwagon of the Iraq war and second by promising that democratic progress in the Middle East would reduce the terrorist threat Americans face at home and abroad.[2] If the hope of reducing anti-American terrorism were the only justification, or even the main one, for an American push to promote Arab democracy, then a single terrorist attack perpetrated by an Arab on an American target would suffice to undermine public support for this drastic and risky change in U.S. policy. If the public's understanding of Middle East democracy promotion is that it is part of a homeland security strategy, then only a few attacks will be enough for the public to conclude that the policy has failed, or at least that it has not succeeded adequately to justify its continuance. Rooting the argument for Arab democracy promotion in a hypothesis about counterterrorism is a recipe for eroding public support.

Instead, Americans should be encouraged to understand the deeper and more enduring interests that have long driven U.S. policy in the Middle East and that drive this change in policy today. Americans understand that stability in the oil-rich Persian Gulf region is crucial to the health of the global economy and their lifestyles at home. But Americans need to be educated about the ways in which the Middle East itself has changed over the years. The vision of fat sheiks, pockets stuffed with petrodollars, spending lavishly on haute couture and racehorses is still an American stereotype, now joined by the scruffy, shouting suicide bomber and the passive victim of the Iraq war. By contrast, unemployment in Saudi Arabia, sectarian tensions in Bahrain, and disputes between violent and non-violent Islamists in Jordan are realities unobserved, much less understood, by the average American.

Traditionally, the promotion of democracy has been one of the goals advanced by American leaders in order to mobilize public support on behalf of overseas engagements. Today an American leader who recognizes the imperative of advancing democracy in the Middle East will have to begin an uphill climb to persuade the American public that the game is worth the candle.

Rebuilding an American consensus in favor of the strategic imperative to help Arabs build a democratic future will require, first, rebuilding bipartisan consensus on behalf of this goal in Congress and between that body and the executive branch. In particular, Congress must reclaim its traditional role as a champion of human rights abroad. In a recent speech, Senator Richard Lugar argued that "in my judgment, foreign policy has more often suffered from a lack of Congressional engagement than from excessive meddling. Members of Congress know too little about the world and are too hesitant to speak about it with their constituents."[3]

But Congress has, at times in the recent past, played a crucial role in advancing human rights and democracy and in giving teeth to American democracy promotion. Congress, as a representative body held electorally accountable more frequently than the president, can help assuage administration concerns about public support for specific policies. Moreover, Congress, when it is functioning well, can undertake policy initiatives that are bipartisan from the beginning, defending a policy against suspicions of narrow or ideological motivations and defending it, too, against radical shifts in the wake of a change in the White House. When implementing a policy with as long a time frame as democracy promotion in the Middle East, such advantages are significant.

The congressional role in human rights and democracy advocacy began to wane with the end of the cold war and the departure of many in the generation of members of Congress who had served in World War II, had direct experience with European tyranny, and had experience in funding democracy promotion in the hostile environment of the Soviet bloc. The linking in the public mind of democracy promotion with the war in Iraq has more recently reduced the incentive for members of Congress from either party to be vocal champions of Arab democracy. Another factor is a change in the way House committee chairmanships are determined and how often they change hands. Members of Congress cannot now remain in one chairmanship for years on end, developing issue expertise and institutional memory.

Instead, shorter-term chairmen bring their own priorities and their own staffs to the job, along with steep learning curves.

But champions can still be found in Congress who care about the fate of the Middle East and about human rights globally. Effective congressional voices can stiffen the spine of an administration that might be ambivalent about pressing democratic demands in a given case. The congressional threat of harsh sanctions produced a much tougher American policy toward apartheid South Africa than Ronald Reagan's administration would have taken if left to itself.[4] Congress's role as "bad cop" can serve not only to stiffen the president's resolve but also to allow the administration to use congressional displeasure as a pressure tactic in discussions with autocratic allies. This good cop, bad cop approach was useful in achieving agreements over economic reform with Egypt in recent years. As Egypt's economic aid allocation from Congress declines, however, Congress's leverage will decline likewise.

Finally, congressional understanding and patience will be necessary to support U.S.-government-funded democracy assistance projects in the Middle East. In a tight budget environment, Congress has become accustomed to demanding evidence of the effects of foreign assistance projects before renewing or increasing funding. Democracy assistance, however, might be unable to demonstrate tangible effects in the near term and also requires flexibility in application to respond to new opportunities when they arise. Congressional funders must be sensitive to and respectful of these needs.

Some readers may conclude this volume little moved, on its central thesis, from where they stood when they began it. To some, the notion that the United States can wield its influence in the world to alter the internal conditions of other countries for the better may still seem naïve and dangerously arrogant. But at the least those who close this book maintaining this view will be inescapably aware of what the United States will risk should it adopt such a view as policy. The Arab states of the Middle East are no longer at equilibrium; they can no longer simply muddle through. Of all the possible forms of political and social change that might sweep the Middle East in coming years, liberalizing, democratizing change is by far the best option.

America's military, economic, and cultural influence is unsurpassed in the world, and despite popular Arab sentiment against U.S. foreign policy, it is unsurpassed in the Middle East as well. Given this reality, the United

States will have a profound influence on the future of this region, whether or not it chooses to direct that influence in a deliberate manner. And because of America's overwhelming influence, it is likely to be implicated in the outcomes of regional change whether or not it has taken conscious steps to affect them. America cannot avoid responsibility for the influence it has; it remains only to choose how that influence will be wielded. One attitude toward the question of America's role in promoting Arab democracy, therefore, cannot survive the preceding analysis: indifference.

Notes

Chapter One

1. For a review of the debate, see Ibrahim Karawan, "Liberalization or Not?" *Freedom Review* 26, no. 2 (1995): 31–33.

2. For a selection of explanations of the persistence of Arab authoritarianism, see, among others, Gwenn Okruhlik, "Rentier Wealth, Unruly Law, and the Rise of Opposition: The Political Economy of Oil States," *Comparative Politics* 31, no. 3 (1999): 295–315; Larry Diamond, Marc F. Plattner, and Daniel Brumberg, eds., *Islam and Democracy in the Middle East* (Johns Hopkins University Press, 2003); David Garnham and Mark Tessler, eds., *Democracy, War, and Peace in the Middle East* (Indiana University Press, 1995); Larbi Sadiki, "To Export or Not to Export Democracy to the Arab World: The Islamist Perspective," *Arab Studies Journal* 6, no. 1 (1998): 60–75; Simon Bromley, "Middle East Exceptionalism: Myth or Reality?" in *Democratization,* edited by David Goldblatt and others (Malden, Mass.: Polity Press, 1997); Rex Brynen, Bahgat Korany, and Paul Noble, eds., *Political Liberalization and Democratization in the Arab World,* vol. 1: *Theoretical Perspectives* (Boulder, Colo.: Lynne Rienner, 1995); Farhad Kazemi, "The Inclusion Imperative," *Middle East Studies Association Bulletin* 30, no. 2 (1996): 147–53; Ghassan Salamé, *Democracy without Democrats? The Renewal of Politics in the Muslim World* (New York: I. B. Tauris, 1994); Eva Bellin, "The Robustness of Authoritarianism in the Middle East: Exceptionalism in Comparative Perspective," *Comparative Politics* 36, no. 2 (2004): 139–57; Daniel Brumberg, "Democratization in the Arab World: The Trap of Liberalized Autocracy," *Journal of Democracy* 13, no. 4 (2002): 56–68; Tim Niblock, "Democratization: A Theoretical and Practical Debate," *British Journal of Middle Eastern Studies* 25, no. 2 (1998): 221–33; Henri Barkey, "Can the Middle East Compete?" *Journal of Democracy* 6, no. 2 (1995): 113–27; Larry Diamond, *Promoting Democracy in the 1990s: Actors and Instruments, Issues and Imperatives* (Washington: Carnegie Commission on Preventing Deadly Conflict, Carnegie Corporation of New York, 1995); Sheila Carapico, "Foreign Aid for Promoting Democracy in the Arab World," *Middle East Journal* 56, no. 3 (2002): 379–96; Lisa Anderson, "Arab Democracy: Dismal Prospects," *World*

Policy Journal 18, no. 3 (2001): 53–61; Augustus Richard Norton, "Political Liberalization and Democratization in the Arab World, vol. 1: Theoretical Perspectives," *American Political Science Review* 90, no. 4 (1996): 933–34; Jill Crystal, "Authoritarianism and Its Adversaries in the Arab World," *World Politics* 46, no. 2 (1994): 262–89; Elie Kedourie, *Democracy and Arab Political Culture* (London: Frank Cass, 1994); and Marsha Pripstein Posusney and Michele Penner Angrist, *Authoritarianism in the Middle East: Regimes and Resistance* (Boulder, Colo.: Lynne Rienner, 2005).

3. Bahrain holds elections for parliament; Oman and the United Arab Emirates hold elections for a limited "consultative council"; and Qatar, at press time, was preparing for its first council elections.

4. Of course, the biggest change in Arab politics in recent years was the forcible ouster of Saddam Hussein from Baghdad in April 2003. The reverberations of that event for Arab democracy are significant, to be sure—and its effects are by no means unidirectional. Indeed, the ultimate effect of Saddam's removal from power on democratic prospects in the Middle East may not be clear for many years. But as I discuss later, the mechanism and consequences of his ouster may be distinguished analytically from the *fact* of his ouster in their effects on regional politics. The latter is, in my view, a clear benefit to aspiring democrats in the Arab world and their allies abroad.

5. Anna Gawel, "Qatari Emir Touts Democracy at Doha Conference," *Washington Diplomat's Diplomatic Pouch,* May 11, 2006 (www.washdiplomat.com/DPouch/2006/May/051106news.html#Anchor5).

6. "Tunis Declaration of 16th Arab Summit," Tunis, Tunisia, 2004 (www.saudi embassy.net/2004News/Statements/StateDetail.asp?cIndex=421).

7. George W. Bush, "Commencement Address at the United States Military Academy in West Point, New York" (June 1, 2002), in *Public Papers of the Presidents of the United States: George W. Bush, 2002* (Washington: Government Printing Office, 2004) p. 921.

8. George W. Bush, "Remarks at the American Enterprise Institute Dinner" (February 26, 2003), in *Public Papers of the Presidents of the United States: George W. Bush, 2003* (Washington: Government Printing Office, 2006), p. 218.

9. George W. Bush, "Inaugural Address" (January 20, 2005), *Weekly Compilation of Presidential Documents* 41, no. 3 (January 24, 2005): 74.

10. George W. Bush, "Remarks on the War on Terror" (March 8, 2005), *Weekly Compilation of Presidential Documents* 41, no. 10 (March 14, 2005): 386.

11. See Roy Godson, "Transstate Security," in *Security Studies for the 21st Century,* edited by Richard H. Schultz Jr., Roy Godson, and George H. Quester (Washington: Brassey's, 1997), pp. 81–130.

12. Tamara Cofman Wittes, "Mass Refugee Flows: Challenges for State Sovereignty and Human Rights," paper presented at the annual meeting of the International Studies Association, Toronto, Canada, March 21, 1997.

13. Sgt. 1st Class Kathleen T. Rhem, "Rumsfeld on Terrorists: Drain the Swamp They Live In," American Forces Press Service, September 18, 2001.

14. Shibley Telhami and James Steinberg, "Fighting Binladenism," in *The Road Ahead: Middle East Policy in the Bush Administration's Second Term,* edited by Flynt Leverett (Saban Center for Middle East Policy, Brookings, 2005).

15. For friends of this theory, see Ariel Cohen, "Promoting Freedom and Democracy:

Fighting the War of Ideas against Islamic Terrorism," *Comparative Strategy* 22, no. 3 (2003): 207–21; David Frum and Richard Perle, *An End to Evil: How to Win the War on Terror* (New York: Random House, 2004); Sean Hannity, *Deliver Us from Evil: Defeating Terrorism, Despotism, and Liberalism* (New York: HarperCollins, 2004); Natan Sharansky and Ron Dermer, *The Case for Democracy: The Power of Freedom to Overcome Tyranny and Terror* (New York: Public Affairs, 2004); and Jennifer Windsor, "Promoting Democratization Can Combat Terrorism," *Washington Quarterly* 26, no. 3 (2003): 43–58. On the speculativeness of this position, see F. Gregory Gause III, "Can Democracy Stop Terrorism?" *Foreign Affairs* 84, no. 5 (2005): 62–76; Henry A. Crumpton, Paula J. Dobriansky, and F. Gregory Gause III, "Tyranny and Terror," *Foreign Affairs* 85, no. 1 (2006): 135–38; and Daniel Byman, *The Five Front War: The Better Way to Fight Global Jihad* (Hoboken, N.J.: John Wiley and Sons, 2007), pp. 157–72.

16. Edward D. Mansfield and Jack Snyder, *Electing to Fight: Why Emerging Democracies Go to War* (MIT Press, 2005).

17. Michael McFaul, "Democracy Promotion as a World Value," *Washington Quarterly* 28, no. 1 (2004–05): 147–63.

18. Bush, "Remarks at the American Enterprise Institute Dinner," pp. 216–20.

19. Tamara Cofman Wittes, "Loose Sovereignty: Political Realities, Shifting Norms, and the Legal Right to Humanitarian Intervention," unpublished manuscript, 1997.

20. Petition to Bashar al-Assad, May 17, 2003, translated and distributed by the Middle East Media Research Institute, Washington, as Special Dispatch Series no. 523.

21. When asked "Which of the following is your biggest concern about the consequences of the war in Iraq?" 42 percent of Arab respondents said they feared that "Iraq will remain unstable and spread instability in the region." When asked "Did the war in Iraq bring more or less democracy in the Middle East?" 69 percent of respondents said it brought less democracy. When posed the question "The U.S. has been actively advocating the spread of democracy in the Middle East especially since the Iraq war. Do you believe that: [democracy is an] important U.S. objective—will make a difference; [democracy is an] important U.S. objective—U.S. doing it the wrong way; or democracy is not a real U.S. objective," 65 percent of respondents said that democracy was not a real U.S. objective. Shibley Telhami, "2006 Annual Arab Public Opinion Survey" (College Park: Anwar Sadat Chair for Peace and Development, University of Maryland, and Zogby International, 2006) (www.bsos.umd.edu/SADAT/2006%20Arab%20Public%20Opinion%20Survey.ppt).

22. Bush, "Inaugural Address."

Chapter Two

1. Thomas Jefferson, "Letter to Roger C. Weightman," Ashbrook Center for Public Affairs at Ashland University (www.ashbrook.org/constitution/roger_weightman.html).

2. Tony Smith and John Ikenberry, "Introduction," in *American Democracy Promotion: Impulses, Strategies, and Impacts,* edited by Michael Cox, G. John Ikenberry, and Takashi Inoguchi (Oxford University Press, 2000), p. 10. Also see the essays in part two of the book.

3. Many scholars and policy experts condemn this American predisposition, on a variety of grounds. Realists reject any value considerations in the determination of foreign policy because they believe it leads to wishful thinking, misapprehension of the international scene, and imprudent policies. Others, especially recently, caution that in a unipolar world America's idealist legacy threatens to pull the United States into an imperial posture vis-à-vis the developing world, provoking resentment and anti-Americanism, which facilitates further terrorism against us. For some expositions of these views, see John Maxwell Hamilton and John Schell, "An Imperial Moment," *Nation* 275, no. 22 (2002): 16–17; G. John Ikenberry, "Illusions of Empire: Defining the New American Order," *Foreign Affairs* 83, no. 2 (2004): 144–54; Michael Mann, *Incoherent Empire* (New York: Verso, 2003); Randall Schweller, "US Democracy Promotion: Realist Reflections," in *American Democracy Promotion,* edited by Cox, Ikenberry, and Inoguchi, pp. 41–62; and Dimitri K. Simes, "America's Imperial Dilemma," *Foreign Affairs* 82, no. 6 (2003): 91–102.

4. Jeane J. Kirkpatrick, "Dictatorships and Double Standards," *Commentary,* November 1979, p. 35.

5. Aryeh Neier, "The New Double Standard," *Foreign Policy* 105 (1997): 91–102.

6. Among the loudest of these skeptics are Noam Chomsky, *Deterring Democracy* (New York: Verso, 1992); William I. Robinson, *Promoting Polyarchy: Globalization, US Intervention, and Hegemony* (Cambridge University Press, 1996); Schweller, "US Democracy Promotion"; and William I. Robinson, "What to Expect from U.S. 'Democracy Promotion' in Iraq," *New Political Science* 26, no. 3 (2004): 441–47.

7. Simes, "America's Imperial Dilemma." Less magnanimous versions of this concern are voiced in Hamilton and Schell, "An Imperial Moment"; and Michael Ignatieff, "Who Are Americans to Think That Freedom Is Theirs to Spread?" *New York Times Magazine,* June 26, 2005, pp. 42–47. See also the books discussed in Ikenberry, "Illusions of Empire."

8. See Rachel Bronson, *Thicker than Oil: The U.S. and Saudi Arabia, a History* (Oxford University Press, 2005); Thomas Lippman, *Inside the Mirage: America's Fragile Partnership with Saudi Arabia* (New York: Basic Books, 2004); and Rachel Bronson, "Understanding U.S.-Saudi Relations," in *Saudi Arabia in the Balance: Political Economy, Society, Foreign Affairs,* edited by Paul Aarts and Gerd Nonneman (London: Hurst, 2005), pp. 372–98. That embargo ultimately proved as painful for the Saudis as for the United States and redoubled their subsequent commitment to price stability. See Christopher Dickey, "The Once and Future Petro Kings: Saudi Oil Clout Isn't What It Used to Be. But the Sheiks Still Control the World's Main Energy Faucet—and They Still Use Their Power Mainly as a Force for Stability," *Newsweek,* April 8, 2002, pp. 38ff.

9. Madeleine Albright and Vin Weber, "The Right Path to Arab Democracy," *Washington Post,* June 8, 2005, p. A21; John McCain, "Security in the Middle East: New Challenges for the US and Europe," *Hampton Roads International Security Quarterly* 2 (2005): 12–15.

10. Philippe C. Schmitter, Guillermo O'Donnell, and Laurence Whitehead, eds., *Transitions from Authoritarian Rule: Prospects for Democracy* (Johns Hopkins University Press, 1986); Guillermo O'Donnell and Philippe C. Schmitter, *Transitions from Authoritarian*

Rule: Tentative Conclusions about Uncertain Democracies (Johns Hopkins University Press, 1986).

11. Edward D. Mansfield and Jack Snyder, *Electing to Fight: Why Emerging Democracies Go to War* (MIT Press, 2005).

12. Daniel Byman, *The Five Front War: The Better Way to Fight Global Jihad* (Hoboken, N.J.: John Wiley and Sons, 2007), pp. 157–72.

13. Ray Takeyh, "Uncle Sam in the Arab Street," *National Interest,* Spring 2004, pp. 45–51.

14. Private conversation with former U.S. government official, spring 2007. Egyptian government officials have also told me on several occasions that political conditions placed on America's economic (not military) aid allocation to Egypt might lead the Egyptian government to reject the package outright.

15. Ray Takeyh, for example, writes that "the case of Saudi Arabia is especially troubling. A nation with a small population base of 24 million and the largest reserves of petroleum in the world (26 percent of proven reserves) is suffering from a 25 percent unemployment rate and a persistent economic recession. At a time when 42 percent of Saudi citizens are under the age of 14, such inefficiency and mismanagement may soon confront the region with an explosive revolutionary problem." Takeyh, "Uncle Sam in the Arab Street," pp. 45–51.

16. Takeyh, "Uncle Sam in the Arab Street"; F. Gregory Gause III, "Beware of What You Wish For," Foreign Affairs.org, February 8, 2006 (www.foreignaffairs.org/2006 0208faupdate85177/f-gregory-gause-iii/beware-of-what-you-wish-for.html).

17. For a discussion of the 1953 coup and its consequences, see Kenneth M. Pollack, *The Persian Puzzle: The Conflict between Iran and America* (New York: Random House, 2004).

18. Kirkpatrick, "Dictatorships and Double Standards."

19. Associated Press, "Algeria Declares Emergency and Postpones Voting," *New York Times,* June 5, 1991, p. A15; Youssef M. Ibrahim, "Algeria's Leader Quits, Citing Fear of Political Chaos," *New York Times,* January 12, 1992, p. A1; Martin Stone, *The Agony of Algeria* (Columbia University Press, 1997), p. 1.

20. William Lowther, Andrew Bilski, and Glen Allen, "Islam's Broadening Sweep," *Maclean's,* January 27, 1992, p. 21.

21. Youssef M. Ibrahim, "Militant Muslims Win Algerian Vote by a Wide Margin," *New York Times,* December 28, 1991, p. A1.

22. Edward P. Djerejian, "The US and the Middle East in a Changing World," address presented at Meridian House International, Washington, June 2, 1992.

23. After Muslim Brotherhood members staged a military-style demonstration at al-Azhar University in Cairo in late 2006, the government suggested that the group was reviving its "old military wing" in an effort to establish "a new Islamic caliphate." Cited in Adam Morrow and Khaled Al-Omrani, "Egypt: Mubarek Blames Brotherhood for Egypt's Economic Unrest," Inter Press Service, January 23, 2007.

24. Quoted in Ken Silverstein, "Parties of God: The Bush Doctrine and the Rise of Islamic Democracy," *Harper's,* March 2007, p. 38.

25. One analyst noted that the sole exception to Washington's global promotion of human rights and democracy was "any country where Islam is the winner of a democratic

election." Robin Wright, "Islam, Democracy and the West," *Foreign Affairs* 71, no. 3 (1992): 137.

26. Silverstein, "Parties of God," p. 34.

27. The sole exception was George H. W. Bush's insistence, upon restoring the Kuwaiti monarchy to power in 1991, that the emir agree to reconvene parliament and henceforth to hold to constitutional procedures protecting the legislative body. This nod to democracy was the result of pressures from Kuwaiti dissidents, who forced additional concessions from the monarchy and have helped Kuwaiti politics to advance significantly toward democracy in the years since the restoration.

28. For more on U.S. Middle East policy during the 1990s, see Martin Indyk, *Innocents Abroad: Lessons from the 1990s for America's Middle East Diplomacy* (New York: Alfred A. Knopf, forthcoming).

29. William B. Quandt, "Algeria," in *The Pivotal States: A New Framework for U.S. Policy in the Developing World,* edited by Emily Hill, Robert Chase, and Paul Kennedy (New York: W. W. Norton, 1999), p. 211.

30. William M. Daley, "Peace and Prosperity: U.S. Priorities for the Middle East," U.S. Embassy, Tel Aviv, October 27, 1997 (http://telaviv.usembassy.gov/publish/peace/archives/1997/me1027a.html).

31. Robert H. Pelletreau, "Developments in the Middle East," *U.S. Department of State Dispatch Magazine* 7, no. 26 (1996): 336–41.

32. Thomas Carothers, *Aiding Democracy Abroad: The Learning Curve* (Washington: Carnegie Endowment for International Peace, 1999).

33. U.S. efforts to promote democracy in the former Soviet states have been criticized for many of the same reasons as today's democratization programs in the Middle East. Thomas Carothers pointed out the main criticisms of U.S. democracy promotion programs in the former Soviet Union and eastern Europe: too much money goes to American organizations rather than to people in the target countries; aid is often concentrated in large, top-down programs; and aid is often based on U.S.-oriented, predetermined models rather than adapted to local environments. Recipient countries have also expressed criticisms of things such as pressure from aid officials to come up with quantifiable measures of progress and anecdotes of success to persuade Congress that the money was well-spent. Thomas Carothers, "Aiding Post-Communist Societies: A Better Way?" *Problems of Post-Communism* 43, no. 5 (September–October 1996): 15–24.

34. "In 18 of 21 Countries Polled, Most See Bush's Reelection as Negative for World Security" (London: BBC World Service and GlobeScan, 2005) (www.globescan.com/news_archives/bbcpoll.html); "U.S. Image Up Slightly, but Still Negative: American Character Gets Mixed Reviews" (Washington: Pew Global Attitudes Project, 2005) (http://pewglobal.org/reports/display.php?ReportID=247).

35. "Islamic Extremism Common Concern for Muslim and Western Publics: Support for Terror Wanes Among Muslim Publics" (Washington: Pew Global Attitudes Project, 2005) (http://pewglobal.org/reports/display.php?ReportID=248); John Zogby and James Zogby, "Impressions of America: How Arabs View America, How Arabs Learn About America," Zogby International, Washington, 2004 (www.arabvoices.net/2004_impressions_of_america_poll.pdf); Shibley Telhami, "2006 Annual Arab Public Opinion Survey" (College Park: Anwar Sadat Chair for Peace and Development, University of Maryland,

and Zogby International, 2006) (www.bsos.umd.edu/SADAT/2006%20Arab%20 Public%20Opinion%20Survey.ppt).

36. Thomas Carothers, "U.S. Democracy Promotion during and after Bush," Carnegie Endowment for International Peace, Washington, 2007; Takeyh, "Uncle Sam in the Arab Street."

37. Telhami, "2006 Annual Arab Public Opinion Survey."

Chapter Three

1. Quoted in Jeffrey Goldberg, "Breaking Ranks: What Turned Brent Scowcroft Against the Bush Administration?" *New Yorker,* October 31, 2005, p. 60.

2. Primary among those making this argument are Jon B. Alterman, "Iraq and Beyond: Challenges of Transatlantic Cooperation in the Middle East," paper presented at the International Conference on the Challenges of the Transatlantic Agenda and the Prospects of U.S.-Italy Cooperation, Rome, June 11, 2007; F. Gregory Gause III, "Sovereignty, Statecraft, and Stability in the Middle East," *Journal of International Affairs* 45, no. 2 (1992): 441–67; and F. Gregory Gause III, "Revolutionary Fevers and Regional Contagion: Domestic Structures and the 'Export' of Revolution in the Middle East," *Journal of South Asian and Middle Eastern Studies* 14, no. 3 (1991): 1–23.

3. Gause, "Revolutionary Fevers and Regional Contagion," p. 10.

4. See Michael Hudson, *Arab Politics: The Search for Legitimacy* (Yale University Press, 1979); and Bassam Tibi, *Arab Nationalism: A Critical Enquiry* (New York: St. Martin's, 1981). Lisa Anderson argued that "'nationalists' had come to be a term of elegant ambiguity, denoting opposition to European rule and connoting loyalties as various as the Muslim community of the faithful, the Arab cultural world, and the local state. While the nationalists were contesting European rule, these ambiguous connotations mattered little, but as the countries of the Middle East reached independence, the bases on which governments would claim legitimacy became a major preoccupation." Lisa Anderson, "Religion and State in Libya: The Politics of Identity," *Annals of the American Academy of Political and Social Science* 483 (1986): 64–65. Abbas Kelidar argued that the political structure of Iraq, Syria, Lebanon, and Jordan was "as alien and artificial as the boundaries drawn to demarcate their international frontiers" and that such a situation had "rendered the emergence of a political community with a single focus of loyalty and allegiance difficult, if not impossible." Abbas Kelidar, "States without Foundations: The Political Evolution of State and Society in the Arab East," *Journal of Contemporary History* 28, no. 2 (1993): 315.

5. Saad Eddin Ibrahim, "Reviving Middle Eastern Liberalism," *Journal of Democracy* 14, no. 4 (2003): 9–10.

6. Albert Hourani, *A History of the Arab Peoples* (Harvard University Press, 1991), pp. 310, 324–28.

7. Ibid., p. 403.

8. "Mubarak Son Hits Out at U.S. Ambitions for Mideast," Agence France-Presse, September 19, 2006.

9. William R. Polk, *The Arab World Today* (Harvard University Press, 1991), p. 212.

10. Hourani, *A History of the Arab Peoples,* p. 411.

11. On corporatist authoritarianism in the Middle East, see, among others, Nazih N. Ayubi, *Overstating the Arab State: Politics and Society in the Middle East* (London: I. B. Tauris, 1995); and Rex Brynen, Bahgat Korany, and Paul Noble, eds., *Political Liberalization and Democratization in the Arab World,* vol. 1: *Theoretical Perspectives* (Boulder, Colo.: Lynne Rienner, 1995).

12. Samuel P. Huntington, "The Clash of Civilizations and the Remaking of World Order," *Foreign Affairs* 72, no. 3 (1993): 40; Samuel P. Huntington, "Will More Countries Become Democratic?" *Political Science Quarterly* 99, no. 2 (1984): 214. Others noting the apparent hostility of Islam toward democracy include Elie Kedourie, *Democracy and Arab Political Culture* (London: Frank Cass, 1994); and Howard J. Wiarda, *Cracks in the Consensus: Debating the Democracy Agenda in U.S. Foreign Policy* (Washington: Center for Strategic and International Studies, 1997).

13. Russell H. Fitzgibbon, "Pathology of Democracy in Latin America: A Political Scientist's Point of View," *American Political Science Review* 44, no. 1 (1950): 118–29; Arthur P. Whitaker, "Pathology of Democracy in Latin America: A Historian's Point of View," *American Political Science Review* 44, no. 1 (1950): 101–18; Li Chenyang, *The Tao Encounters the West: Explorations in Comparative Philosophy* (State University of New York Press, 1999).

14. King Fahd, quoted in John L. Esposito, ed., *Oxford History of Islam* (Oxford University Press, 1999), p. 677; Fareed Zakaria, "Culture Is Destiny: A Conversation with Lee Kuan Yew," *Foreign Affairs* 73, no. 2 (1994): 109–26.

15. Larry Diamond, Marc F. Plattner, and Daniel Brumberg, eds., *Islam and Democracy in the Middle East* (Johns Hopkins University Press, 2003).

16. Lisa Anderson, "Liberalism, Islam, and the Arab State," *Dissent,* Fall 1994, p. 440.

17. Terry Lynn Karl, *The Paradox of Plenty: Oil Booms and Petro-States* (University of California Press, 1997).

18. Energy Information Administration, "Opec and Non-Opec Oil Export Revenue Spreadsheet" (Department of Energy, 2005).

19. On the Saudi welfare system and its relationship to oil rents and political structures, see Paul Aarts and Gerd Nonneman, eds., *Saudi Arabia in the Balance: Political Economy, Society, Foreign Affairs* (London: Hurst, 2005); and Daryl Champion, *The Paradoxical Kingdom: Saudi Arabia and the Momentum of Reform* (Columbia University Press, 2003).

20. Jeremy M. Sharp, *Egypt–United States Relations* (Washington: Congressional Research Service, 2005).

21. See Gause, "Sovereignty, Statecraft, and Stability in the Middle East" and "Revolutionary Fevers and Regional Contagion."

22. "World Development Indicators" (World Bank, 2007). The Arab countries for which reliable data were available were Algeria, Bahrain, Egypt, Jordan, Kuwait, Lebanon, Libya, Morocco, Oman, Saudi Arabia, Syria, Tunisia, the United Arab Emirates, and Yemen.

23. Abu Ahmad Mustafa (pseudonym), "When Will the Arabs Learn the Lesson, Just Once?" *al-Sharq al-Awsat,* May 8, 2002, published in English in "An Arab Diplomat on the Leadership Crisis in the Arab World," Special Dispatch Series 540, July 22, 2003 (Washington: Middle East Media Research Institute).

24. This baby boom can be attributed largely to advances in basic health care in the post-independence period, which significantly reduced infant mortality. In a few countries,

such as Saudi Arabia, the government's provision of services has encouraged a greater number of children per family.

25. United Nations Development Program, *Human Development Report 2006* (New York: Palgrave Macmillan, 2006) (http://hdr.undp.org/statistics/data/indic/indic_44_1_1.html).

26. United Nations Development Program, *Arab Human Development Report 2002: Creating Opportunities for Future Generations* (New York: United Nations, 2002), p. 38.

27. Graham E. Fuller, "The Youth Factor: The New Demographics of the Middle East and the Implications for U.S. Policy," Saban Center Analysis Paper 3 (Brookings, June 2003), p. 6.

28. Tarik M. Yousef, "Development, Growth and Policy Reform in the Middle East and North Africa since 1950," *Journal of Economic Perspectives* 18, no. 3 (2004): 91–116; United Nations Development Program, *Arab Human Development Report 2004: Towards Freedom in the Arab World* (New York: United Nations, 2005). According to the World Bank's review of world development indicators, the percentage of the labor force unemployed in Algeria was 20.1 (2004), in Egypt, 11.0 (2003), in Iraq, 26.8 (2004), in Morocco, 11.9 (2003), and in the West Bank and Gaza, 26.8 (2004). These were the most recent years for which data were available.

29. Yousef, "Development, Growth and Policy Reform." Moreover, the region has to create those new jobs without the rapid macroeconomic development and large national infrastructure projects that provided employment for many people over the past fifty years.

30. Ibid.

31. In 2002 there were 1.33 times as many noncitizens as citizens in the labor forces of Bahrain, Saudi Arabia, Oman, Qatar, and Kuwait, calculating from figures in *Cooperation Council for the Arab States of the Gulf Statistical Bulletin*, vol. 15 (2006) (http://library.gcc-sg.org/gccstatvol15/toc/index1.htm). On efforts to "localize" the labor force in Kuwait and Saudi Arabia, see "Gulf Bank Achieves High Percentage of Local Staff through Affirmative Action," Middle East Company News Wire, May 15, 2007; and "Saudi Arabia Bans 107 Companies from Employing Foreign Workers," *Arab News*, April 1, 2007 (www.arabnews.com/?page=1&section=0&article=94423&d=1&m=4&y=2007).

32. Fatma El-Hamidi, "The Effects of Structural Adjustment on Youth Unemployment in Egypt," paper presented at the twelfth annual conference of the Economic Research Forum, December 19, 2005; Navtej Dhillon and Tarik Yousef, *Inclusion: Meeting the 100 Million Youth Challenge* (Brookings, 2007).

33. Dhillon and Yousef, *Inclusion.*

34. Steven Heydemann, *Networks of Privilege in the Middle East: The Politics of Economic Reform Revisited* (New York: Palgrave Macmillan, 2004).

35. Gause, "Revolutionary Fevers and Regional Contagion," p. 10.

36. Michael Slackman and Mona el-Naggar, "Testing Egypt, Mubarak Rival Is Sent to Jail," *New York Times*, December 25, 2005, p. A1; Joshua Muravchik, "The Trials of Ayman Nour," *Wall Street Journal*, May 8, 2006, p. 18. Nour's subsequent conviction and sentencing, however, demonstrate the limits of outsiders' ability to affect individual human rights cases. My point is simply that the West is swifter and more explicit in its response to human rights abuses today than in the recent past—not that recognition of abuse will necessarily bring relief to the victims or effective punishment to the perpetrators.

The collective effect of this external scrutiny on repression may be positive, but individual injustices are still all too frequent.

37. Youssef Ibrahim, "Land of Missed Chances," *New York Sun,* April 28, 2006, p. 6.

38. Anthony Shadid, "The War in Iraq: The Iraqi Civilian Perspective," speech presented at the Council on Foreign Relations, New York, March 6, 2006.

39. Of course, responsiveness to public views might in some issue areas lead some regimes to adopt "Arabist" policies on, for example, Palestine. The public feels, for sentimental, religious, and ethnic reasons, as well as because it was socialized to Arabist ideology, that what happens in Palestine matters deeply to it. But for the most part those policies do not affect what actually happens in Palestinian-Israeli relations. And ultimately these same citizens will judge their governments not on their policies toward Israel but on their ability to create jobs and opportunities at home.

40. Johanna McGeary, "Can Al-Qaeda Find a New Nest? To Do Their Worst, Terrorists Need a Sanctuary. The Next Order of Battle Is to Deny Them One," *Time,* December 24, 2001, pp. 50–55; "Saudi Police Foil Smugglers Trying to Bring Weapons from Yemen, Says Press Report," Associated Press Worldstream, December 10, 2005.

41. United Nations Development Program, *Arab Human Development Report 2004;* "Views of a Changing World" (Washington: Pew Global Attitudes Project, 2003) (http://people-press.org/reports/pdf/185.pdf).

42. Michael McFaul, "Democracy Promotion as a World Value," *Washington Quarterly* 28, no. 1 (2004–05): 147–63.

43. See Daniel Brumberg, "Liberalization versus Democracy: Understanding Arab Political Reform," Working Paper 37 (Washington: Carnegie Endowment for International Peace, May 2003).

Chapter Four

1. Off-the-record interview, summer 2004.

2. Navtej Dhillon, "The Wedding Shortage," *Newsweek* (International, Pacific Edition), March 5, 2007, p. 35. See also Navtej Dhillon and Tarik Yousef, *Inclusion: Meeting the 100 Million Youth Challenge* (Brookings, 2007).

3. Valerie M. Hudson and Andrea M. den Boer, *Bare Branches: The Security Implications of Asia's Surplus Male Population* (MIT Press, 2004).

4. Fareed Zakaria, *The Future of Freedom: Illiberal Democracy at Home and Abroad* (New York: Norton, 2003), p. 69.

5. Interview, Cairo, September 2004.

6. Roundtable with senior military officers, Cairo, September 2004.

7. Thomas Carothers, "The Sequencing Fallacy," *Journal of Democracy* 18, no. 1 (2007): 15.

8. Roundtable discussion at the Brookings Institution, March 27, 2006.

9. Richard N. Haass, *The Opportunity: America's Moment to Alter History's Course* (New York: Public Affairs, 2005), p. 72.

10. Zakaria, *The Future of Freedom,* p. 72.

11. Carothers, "The Sequencing Fallacy," p. 15.

12. Ibid, p. 16.

13. Eva Bellin, *Stalled Democracy: Capital, Labor, and the Paradox of State-Sponsored*

Development (Cornell University Press, 2002), pp. 3–4. Bellin provides a complete discussion of Tunisia's failed reform.

14. Afshin Molavi, "Tehran Dispatch: Fine China," *New Republic,* September 8, 2003 (www.tnr.com/doc.mhtml?i=20030908&s=molavi090803). It may be, however, that rapid economic growth in a closed political system such as China's is producing its own sickness: government officials under pressure to show results are putting government loans behind dubious investments, risking the collapse of China's financial sector if these projects fail. See Adam Davidson, "China's Economy May Outgrow Its Environment," *Weekend Edition,* National Public Radio, July 16, 2006 (www.npr.org/templates/story/story.php?storyId=5560807).

15. Saad Eddin Ibrahim, "Reform and Frustration in Egypt," *Journal of Democracy* 7, no. 4 (1996): 129.

16. Interviews in Cairo, June and September 2004.

17. Eberhard Kienle, "More than a Response to Islamism: The Political Deliberalization of Egypt in the 1990s," *Middle East Journal* 52, no. 2 (1998): 221.

18. For more on the failed links between economic and political reform in the region, see Tarik M. Yousef, "Development, Growth, and Policy Reform in the Middle East and North Africa since 1950," *Journal of Economic Perspectives* 18, no. 3 (2004): 91–116.

19. Interviews in Cairo, June 2004; Ibrahim, "Reform and Frustration in Egypt," pp. 125–35.

20. James Glanz, "A Little Democracy or a Genie Unbottled," *New York Times,* January 29, 2006, sec. 4, p. 1.

21. And even in Iraq local leaders compelled the occupying U.S. government to schedule elections far earlier than American plans and preferences dictated. The strength of public demand for elections should not be underestimated.

22. Off-the-record meeting at the National Endowment for Democracy, September 14, 2004.

23. Sameer Jarrah, "The Democratic Transition in Jordan: Freedom of Association as a Case Study," Saban Center Analysis Paper (Brookings, forthcoming); Kareem Elbayar, "NGO Laws in Selected Arab States," *International Journal of Not-for-Profit Law* 7, no. 4 (2005): 3–27.

24. The Broader Middle East and North Africa Intiative (BMENA), though conceived with the Helsinki accords in mind, does not provide the fundamental quid pro quo that Helsinki contained, that of sovereignty protections in exchange for human rights progress. Moreover, it does not bind the Arab states as signatories but treats them as targets or subjects of the initiative.

25. Robert D. Kaplan, "We Can't Force Democracy: Creating Normality Is the Real Mideast Challenge," *Washington Post,* March 2, 2006, p. A21.

26. See Elie Kedourie, *Democracy and Arab Political Culture* (London: Frank Cass, 1994). A similar concern animates Fareed Zakaria's arguments in *The Future of Freedom.*

27. Jon B. Alterman, "The False Promise of Arab Liberals," *Policy Review* 125 (June–July 2004): 77–85.

28. Daniel Brumberg, "Beyond Liberalization?" *Wilson Quarterly* 28, no. 2 (2004): 47–55; Marina Ottaway, "Evaluating Middle East Reform: How Do We Know When It Is Significant?" *Carnegie Papers* 56 (2005).

29. "Jordan's Monarch Accuses Iraq of Involvement in Riots," Agence France-Presse, August 24, 1996.

30. Hassan M. Fattah, "Strong Showing for Opposition Party in Bahrain Elections," *New York Times*, November 27, 2006, p. A3; Hassan M. Fattah, "In Bahrain, a Referendum on Promises," *New York Times*, November 25, 2006, p. A3.

31. Habib Toumi, "Official of US Institute Leaves," *Gulf News*, May 13, 2006 (http://archive.gulfnews.com/articles/06/05/13/10039484.html).

32. Les Campbell, of the National Democratic Institute, personally observed these ballot papers and related his experience at a panel discussion at the School for Advanced International Studies in Washington on October 15, 2007.

Chapter Five

1. Quoted in David Finkel, "U.S. Ideals Meet Reality in Yemen," *Washington Post*, December 18, 2005, p. A1.

2. "Mubarak Leads Opposition to Bush Initiative," Agence France-Presse, February 26, 2004.

3. Mark LeVine, "Chaos, Globalization, and the Public Sphere: Political Struggle in Iraq and Palestine," *Middle East Journal* 60, no. 3 (2006): 467.

4. George W. Bush, speech to the National Defense University, Fort Lesley J. McNair, Washington, March 8, 2005 (www.whitehouse.gov/news/releases/2005/03/20050308-3.html).

5. See Paul Salem, "Lebanon at the Crossroads: Rebuilding an Arab Democracy," Middle East Memo 7 (Saban Center for Middle East Policy, Brookings, May 2005) (www.brookings.edu/articles/2005/0531middleeast_salem.aspx).

6. Office of the United States Trade Representative, "Middle East Free Trade Area Initiative" (www.ustr.gov/Trade_Agreements/Regional/MEFTA/Section_Index.html).

7. Among the Arab states, Algeria, Lebanon, and Yemen were still not WTO members as of 2007.

8. See, for example, Office of the United States Trade Representative, *The President's Trade Policy Agenda*, March 1, 2006, p. 4 (www.ustr.gov/assets/Document_Library/Reports_Publications/2006/2006_Trade_Policy_Agenda/asset_upload_file151_9073.pdf).

9. Steffen Hertog, "The GCC and Arab Economic Integration: A New Paradigm," *Middle East Policy* 14, no. 1 (2007): 52–68.

10. Negotiations with the UAE began in March 2005 but faltered in May 2006 after the Dubai Ports World scandal in Washington (in which a UAE deal to buy a company that managed U.S. port operations was scuppered by congressional opponents who raised the fear of Arab terrorism) led the Emirates, for domestic reasons, to toughen its stance in the talks.

11. Figure taken from Department of State, "FY 2007 Congressional Budget Justification for Foreign Operations" (www.state.gov/documents/organization/60654.pdf). The rationale for MEPI was laid out in a speech in December 2002 by Richard N. Haass, then director of policy planning at the U.S. Department of State. Richard N. Haass, "Toward a Greater Democracy in the Muslim World," Council on Foreign Relations, Washington, December 4, 2002 (www.cfr.org/publication/5300/toward_a_greater_democracy_in_the_muslim_world.html). The program was formally launched later that month by Secretary of State Colin Powell. Colin L. Powell, "The U.S.-Middle East Partner-

ship Initiative: Building Hope for the Years Ahead" (Washington: Heritage Foundation, December 12, 2002) (www.state.gov/secretary/former/powell/remarks/2002/15920.htm).

12. This problem was exacerbated by MEPI's lack of grants staff trained to identify programs worthy of funding and by bureaucratic pressures to spend its congressionally mandated budget quickly in order to justify new funding requests.

13. Tamara Cofman Wittes and Sarah E. Yerkes, "The Middle East Partnership Initiative: Problems, Progress, and Prospects," Middle East Memo 5 (Saban Center for Middle East Policy, Brookings, 2004).

14. Interviews with officials in the Department of State, January and November 2007.

15. Brian Whitaker, "Saudi Women Make Electoral Breakthrough," *The Guardian*, December 1, 2005.

16. For excerpts from several such columns published in 2007 in *al-Riyadh* and *al-Watan*, see "Saudi Women Columnists Protest against Oppression of Women in Saudi Arabia," Special Dispatch Series 1570 (Washington: Middle East Media Research Institute) (www.memri.org/bin/opener.cgi?Page=archives&ID=SP157007).

17. Laura Bush, speech at the Sheikh Khalifa Medical Center, Abu Dhabi, United Arab Emirates, October 22, 2007 (www.state.gov/g/wi/93960.htm).

18. "Bahrain Bans Protests during Reforms Forum," Agence France-Presse, July 29, 2005; Anne Gearan, "Mideast Democracy Summit Ends with No Deal," Associated Press, November 13, 2005. A version of this declaration was finally adopted over Egyptian objections at the Democracy Assistance Dialogue, a smaller and lower-profile gathering of government and NGO representatives, in June 2006 in Sana'a, Yemen.

19. Bush eventually sent (and leaked) a letter to Mubarak informing him that the U.S. government would ask Congress for no additional aid to Egypt while the Ibrahim case remained unresolved. No formal aid request was then pending, although Egypt was expecting an additional allocation in proportion to new aid given to Israel. The threat had an immediate effect, and Ibrahim's case was finally dismissed by a higher court—whose judge took the opportunity granted him to lambaste the government for its shoddy attempt to enforce fraudulent charges.

20. Condoleezza Rice, address at the American University of Cairo, Egypt, June 20, 2005 (www.state.gov/secretary/rm/2005/48328.htm).

21. Peter Baker, "As Democracy Push Falters, Bush Feels Like a 'Dissident,'" *Washington Post*, August 20, 2007, p. A1.

22. George W. Bush, "President Bush Discusses Freedom in Iraq and Middle East," in *20th Anniversary of the National Endowment for Democracy* (Washington: United States Chamber of Commerce, National Endowment for Democracy, 2003).

23. For an account of Gamal Mubarak's White House meeting, see Brian Whitaker, "A Welcome at the White House," May 17, 2006, at http://commentisfree.guardian. co.uk/brian_whitaker/2006/05/a_welcome_at_the_white_house.html.

Chapter Six

1. Fareed Zakaria, *The Future of Freedom* (New York: W. W. Norton, 2003).

2. Quoted in Daniel Williams, "New Vehicle for Dissent Is a Fast Track to Prison; Bloggers Held Under Egypt's Emergency Laws," *Washington Post*, May 31, 2006, p. A10.

3. Off-the-record interview, Cairo, September 2004.

4. For more on this subject, see Martin S. Indyk and Tamara Cofman Wittes, "Back to Balancing in the Middle East," *American Interest* 3, no. 2 (2007): 42–51.

5. The Millennium Challenge Corporation provides large development grants to countries that meet a set of criteria for sound development and economic policies and good governance. Most Arab countries are too wealthy to qualify for Millennium Challenge funds, but the poorest, such as Yemen, do.

6. David Finkel, "In the End, a Painful Choice; Program Weighs Leader's Edict, Tribes' Needs," *Washington Post,* December 20, 2005, p. A1.

7. This reduction was negotiated to accord with a simultaneous reduction in U.S. economic assistance to Israel, despite the widely disparate economic situations in the two countries.

8. Department of State, *Congressional Budget Justification, Foreign Operations, Fiscal Year 2008* (Washington, February 2007), p. 483.

9. See Steven Cook, *Ruling but Not Governing: The Military and Political Development in Egypt, Algeria, and Turkey* (Johns Hopkins University Press, 2007); and Mehran Kamrava, "Military Professionalization and Civil-Military Relations in the Middle East," *Political Science Quarterly* 115, no. 1 (2000): 67–93.

10. Builders for Peace was a group organized by the U.S. government in 1994 and co-chaired by Mel Levine and James Zogby to mobilize private sector investment to support the Oslo peace process and the emergence of Palestinian autonomy. For more information see "Group to Promote U.S. Investment in West Bank," *Washington Post,* December 1, 1993, p. A18.

11. Off-the-record conversation, Cairo, June 2004.

Chapter Seven

1. Yusuf Qaradawi, in an interview with *Newsnight,* BBC Two, July 7, 2004.

2. Judy Barsalou, "Islamists at the Ballot Box: Findings from Egypt, Jordan, Kuwait, and Turkey," United States Institute of Peace, p. 2.

3. Youssef M. Ibrahim, "In Algeria, Clear Plans to Lay Down Islamic Law," *New York Times,* December 31, 1991, p. A10.

4. Barsalou, "Islamists at the Ballot Box."

5. After 2005 this group moved firmly into the *takfiri* camp when it renamed itself al Qaeda of the Islamic Maghreb and reportedly assisted in terrorist attacks in Tunisia.

6. Judith Palmer Harik, *Hezbollah: The Changing Face of Terrorism* (New York: I. B. Tauris, 2004), pp. 48, 52.

7. Martin Kramer, "Islamists of All Kinds," remarks presented at the Center for Strategic and International Studies, Washington, October 24, 2005.

8. Ted Robert Gurr, *Minorities at Risk: A Global View of Ethnopolitical Conflicts* (Washington: United States Institute of Peace Press, 1993); Donald L. Horowitz, *Ethnic Groups in Conflict* (University of California Press, 1985).

9. Omar G. Encarnacion, "Beyond Civil Society: Promoting Democracy after September 11," *Orbis* 47, no. 4 (2003): 705–20.

10. It is worthwhile in this regard to consider the history of other such localized militant groups that eventually made the transition to peaceful politics in non-Muslim

contexts. Two notable examples are the African National Congress and the Irish Republican Army. In both cases the organizations' military demobilization and entrance into
formal politics came as part and parcel of negotiated peace agreements with their rivals.
When a realistic political settlement is on offer alongside a functioning state apparatus,
it further reduces the rationale such groups use to maintain their arms while engaging
in local politics.

11. It is important to distinguish this discussion of whether and how Islamists can be
integrated within democratic Arab politics from the more philosophical question of
whether "Islam" and "democracy" are compatible concepts. Although some writers, such
as Elie Kedourie in his *Democracy and Arab Political Culture* (London: Frank Cass, 1994),
argue that Islam's emphasis on divine sovereignty prevents sincere acceptance of pluralist competitive politics, this question has largely been resolved empirically by the fact
that more than two-thirds of the world's Muslims live today under democratic governments in countries such as Indonesia, India, Turkey, and Bangladesh. In addition, religious scholars and democracy activists alike have come up with a variety of arguments
on behalf of democracy that are firmly situated within the mainstream of Islamic
jurisprudence. My concern is therefore not with the abstract question of Islam's compatibility with democracy but with the more specific question of whether the Islamist
movements extant in today's Arab world can play a constructive role in the democratization, democratic consolidation, and long-term democratic practice of Arab societies in
the years to come.

12. Indeed, some of the most interesting Islamist movements in this third category
emerged from splits within broader movements that experienced state repression and
were given opportunities to reform. For example, the Islamic Action Front in Jordan
emerged when the Muslim Brotherhood debated whether or not to accept King Hussein's offer of electoral participation in exchange for explicit recognition of the legitimacy of the monarchy.

13. Even the Moroccan Party of Justice and Development, often touted by Western
observers as the most moderate and "hopeful" among Arab Islamist movements,
emerged from the merger of two groups, one of which had a violent history.

14. A broader trend is taking place in Arab discourse today in which the term *martyr*
is used to refer to all kinds of dead persons, such as those killed in traffic accidents. This
"defining down" of the term *martyr* has been the subject of recent discussion, both hand-
wringing and cynical, in the Arab press and commentariat.

15. Nathan J. Brown, Amr Hamzawy, and Marina Ottaway, "Islamist Movements and
the Democratic Process in the Arab World: Exploring the Gray Zones," *Carnegie Papers*
67 (2006); Amr Hamzawy, Marina Ottaway, and Nathan J. Brown, "What Islamists Need
to Be Clear About: The Case of the Egyptian Muslim Brotherhood," Carnegie Endowment for International Peace, Washington, 2007.

16. I should note that attitudes toward violence, minorities and women, political pluralism, and the role of religious authority are relevant in assessing the democratic credentials of *all* political movements, not only Islamists. Some of the leftist and nationalist parties of the secular Arab states also display troubling tendencies on some of these
questions. Because leftist parties are generally marginal, and because the core policy concern at issue in this book is the role of Islamist movements, I focus on their attitudes, but
in doing so I do not wish to ignore the need to consider other parties' likely abilities to
embrace these fundamental tenets of liberal democratic politics.

17. Mohamed Elmenshawy, "The Muslim Brotherhood Shows Its True Colors," *Christian Science Monitor,* October 12, 2007, p. 9.

18. Jillian Schwedler, "Democratization, Inclusion, and the Moderation of Islamist Parties," *Development* 50, no. 1 (2007): 60. See also her *Faith in Moderation: Islamist Parties in Jordan and Yemen* (Cambridge University Press, 2006).

19. Mark Tessler, "The Origins of Popular Support for Islamist Movements: A Political Economy Analysis," in *Islam, Democracy, and the State in North Africa,* edited by John Entelis (Indiana University Press, 1997), pp. 93–126. Tessler has 2006 Arab Barometer data supporting the same conclusion; personal communication, June 2007.

20. Off-the-record conversation, Washington, February 2004.

21. In the Palestinian case, however, a U.S. preference to delay the elections would almost certainly have been respected. Whether this delay might have prevented Hamas's victory remains uncertain.

22. The short-lived U.S. dialogue with the Palestine Liberation Organization was initiated when PLO chairman Yasir Arafat made a speech in December 1988 rejecting terrorism and implicitly recognizing Israel's right to exist. The dialogue lasted until June 1990, after an attack on an Israeli beach by a PLO-affiliated group called Arafat's stated commitments into question and the movement failed to respond adequately to American concerns. The United States and the PLO did not have formal contacts again until after the Israeli-PLO Declaration of Principles was initialed in August 1993.

Chapter Eight

1. Flynt Leverett, "Illusion and Reality," *American Prospect* 19, no. 9 (2006); Walter Isaacson, "The Return of the Realists," *Time,* November 20, 2006, p. 39.

2. "Secretary of State Condoleezza Rice argues that the democratic transformation of the Middle East is the only way to guarantee that men do not fly airplanes into buildings. Such rhetoric is overblown." Madeleine K. Albright, "A Realistic Idealism; There's a Right Way to Support Democracy in the Mideast," *Washington Post,* May 8, 2006, p. A19.

3. Richard G. Lugar, "Remarks at NYU's First Annual Bernard and Irene Schwartz Lecture on Congress," address at the Library of Congress, Washington, September 15, 2005 (http://lugar.senate.gov/press/record.cfm?id=246787&&).

4. Pauline H. Baker, "The United States and South Africa: Persuasion and Coercion," in *Honey and Vinegar: Incentives, Sanctions, and Foreign Policy,* edited by Richard N. Haass and Meghan L. O'Sullivan (Brookings, 2000), pp. 95–119.

Index